100 + Poses:
A Playbook From Beginner To Pro!
By Chi Anderson
Copyright 2025 © The Creative Coach LLC
ISBN: 979-8-218-65564-8
Images courtesy of Jamar 'Church' Pinkston

This book is the property of The Creative Coach LLC and is protected by international copyright law. No part of this ebook may be reproduced, distributed, or transmitted in any form or by any means, including photocopying, recording, or other electronic or mechanical methods, without the prior written permission of The Creative Coach LLC except in the case of brief quotations embodied in critical reviews or articles.

For permissions or inquiries, please visit www.thecreativecoachchi.com.

Table of Contents

Dedication...1

Introduction..3

All Eyes On Me...6

Work The Middle..14

Get Me Bodied..36

Sittin' On Top Of The World................................46

Prop It Like It's Hot..64

Baby Got Hacks..74

Conclusion..79

Meet Chi Anderson..80

Dedication

God, I thank you. Thank you for lifting me up at my lowest and loving me through the trials no one knows about. Thank you for blessing me with the gifts I confidently walk in and those I have yet to see come to fruition. Thank you for reminding me of my why during moments of confusion and disparity. Your love is the gift I don't deserve, yet I can always depend on.

To the amazing women who have experienced most (if not all) of my firsts, this first solo book is for y'all! Angela (Mother), Ruth (Grandmother), Annette (Aunt) and Rosalyn (Godmother).

To my A1, thank you for noticing my creative strengths and nudging me to seize every opportunity. The Creative Coach, LLC wouldn't exist without your stern mentorship and encouragement.

To my sister circle — my tribe.
Thank you SO much for covering me in prayer and accepting me in each season of my life — good, bad, or indifferent. You've been right there, always just a phone call or text away. Thank you for your tough love and endless laughs. Thank you for a safe space to just be, say, and do whatever is on my heart. Thank you for being a daily inspiration and showing me what grace and class look like.

Last, but certainly not least — thank you to every supporter who has believed in me and my ministry from the very start. Without you, there's absolutely no me.

Introduction

Hey y'all! Are you tired of feeling like a deer in headlights every time the camera turns your way? Or maybe you're just ready to level up your photo game and finally show the world your best angles - without the awkwardness, the overthinking, or those "where-do-I-put-my-hands" moments? Sound familiar?! Well, you've found yourself in the right place.

As someone who has tons of experience in front of the camera (modeling, acting, and coaching), I know what it takes to get maximum results without a lot of fuss. Now don't get it twisted, I definitely know how to serve for the GAWDS, but there's a time and place for everything, right?

As far back as I can remember, I've always loved being in front of the camera. I credit that to my grandmother who was always front and center with her polaroid and old school camcorder - you know, the one that had the VHS inserts! Ha! I'm telling my age with that one, but it was truly a time! I believe that's what I love most about capturing special moments. It allows you to freeze time and reflect whenever you like.

I think it's safe to say 2020 caught us all by storm. I believe the best creative ideas were birthed and executed while we were forced to be at home, including my own. We began thinking outside of the box and capitalizing from it! To add insult to injury, I was let go from my job. As devastating as being furloughed was, it gave me an opportunity to jump head first into my own creative lane. Back then, I had no idea what that was; thank God for my tribe who saw something in me that I never would have.

Five years ago, I intentionally intruded on the set of a photoshoot simply because I wanted to meet the stylist I'd been fawning over for the last two years. I wasn't sure if I'd be welcomed, but I brought my trusty fanny pack filled with a mirror, boob tape, lotion, and other 'just in case' must-haves! Pulling up to set, I was low-key nervous but once I got out of the car and saw how frazzled the client was, I instantly jumped in to assist (after hugging who I came to meet of course LOL).

Next thing I know, I became the creative director for the shoot - coaching and guiding the client, refining/tossing her garments for that much needed dramatic effect and giving her the reassurance she deserved. It was a beautiful, divine moment.

I got more than I bargained for that day. Not only have I worked with those two influential ladies multiple times, but I learned that there was a need for what I naturally possessed! That was the beginning of an experience that I have yet to see offered by anyone else. Sure, there are others who offer similar services, but I am THE Creative Coach, umm kay! As a natural cheerleader, pouring into others is embedded in my core. Mix that with my true love for modeling and it's an absolute match strategically made just for me!

This book is your ultimate cheat code to mastering easy go-to poses that scream confidence, even if the thought of being in front of the camera gives you anxiety. I'm here to remind you of one thing; you already have what it takes. This guide is just the cherry on top of your fabulous self!

Inside this playbook, you'll find 100+ beginner-friendly poses that are simple, effective, and designed to make you feel fierce from head to toe. Whether you're prepping for headshots, striking full body poses for your brand, adding flair with props, or just flickin' it up with your friends - I've got you covered.

Taking pictures can be both planned and impromptu. Either way, I want you prepared for whatever, whenever, however! Think of this as your personal posing coach (me!) packed into a book, cheering you on from every page.

So, get ready to own your angles, slay your shots, and most importantly, feel good while doing it. Remember, posing is simply your feelings being captured, so dig deep and allow your light to shine bright. Are you ready to step in front of the lens (or your cell phone) with boldness and charisma? Let's werK!

Chi
XOXO

All
Eyes
On
Me

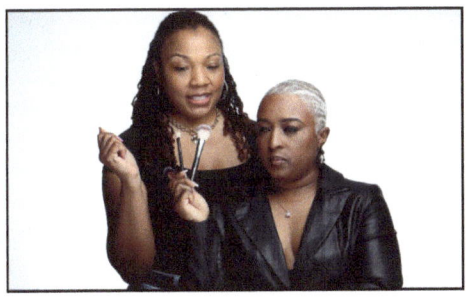

*Headshots are generally done for professional photoshoots (Ex: LinkedIn, company/small business websites), branding, or modeling/talent agencies.

TIP #1 - A standard black, blue, or grey suit jacket with a white button-down shirt is traditionally worn for professional headshots. Honestly, it's more about your face than anything but make sure everything from the chest up is well groomed, clean and ironed. Hair should be simple and neat. Keep makeup natural and jewelry to a minimum.

TIP #2 - Branding shoots are catered towards your business. I will always suggest choosing looks according to the services you offer and your personality. For example, beauty industry professionals tend to wear all black or a statement piece while Estheticians will usually wear scrubs and/or a lab coat. Basically, whatever you would wear to service clients is what you would wear for your branding photoshoot. It's ok to spice it up with splashes of color, accessories, and props if you like!

TIP #3 - A white t-shirt or tank top will always reign supreme when submitting to modeling/talent agencies; labels and busy prints aren't as welcomed. Your hair should be pulled back with little to no makeup. Scouters want you looking straight on so they can check out your facial features, hair, etc. This is no time for posey posing...LOL. Talent agencies tend to welcome smiles while modeling agencies would rather not see your pearly whites as much.

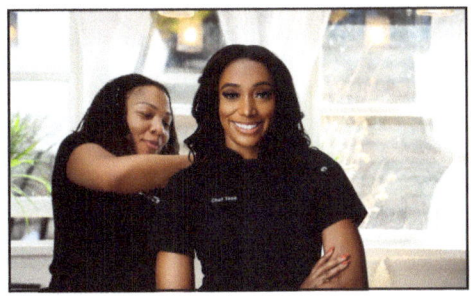

1. Straight On No Smile

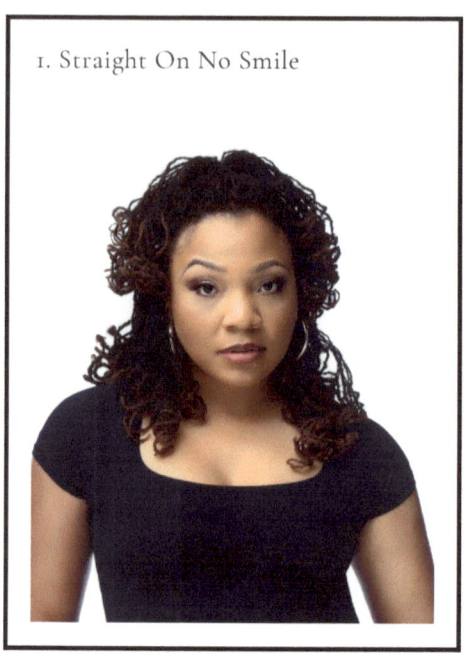

2. Straight On Smiling

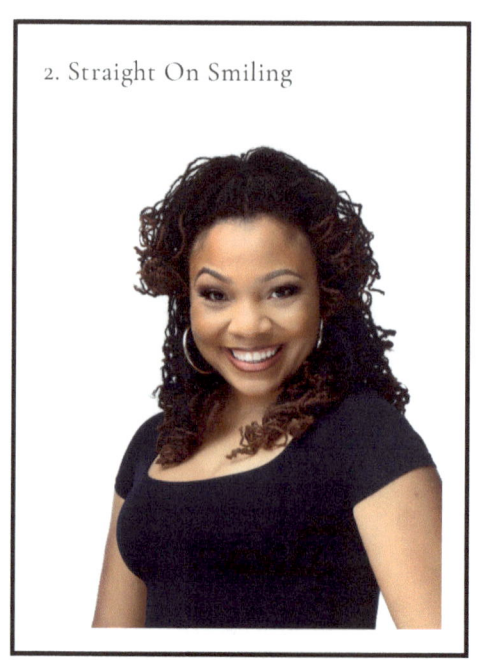

3. Side Eye Left No Smile

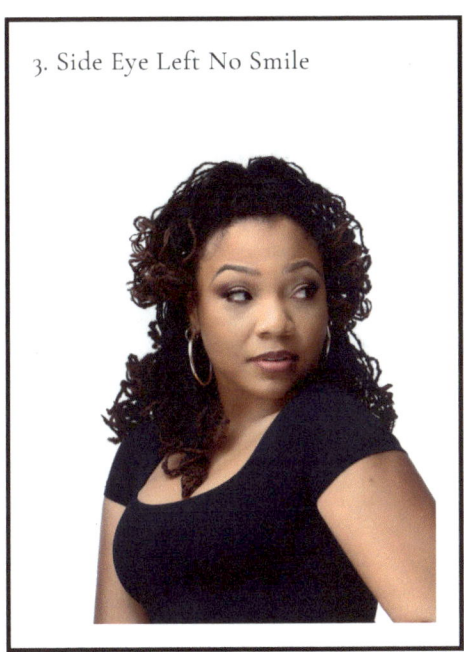

4. Side Eye Left Smiling

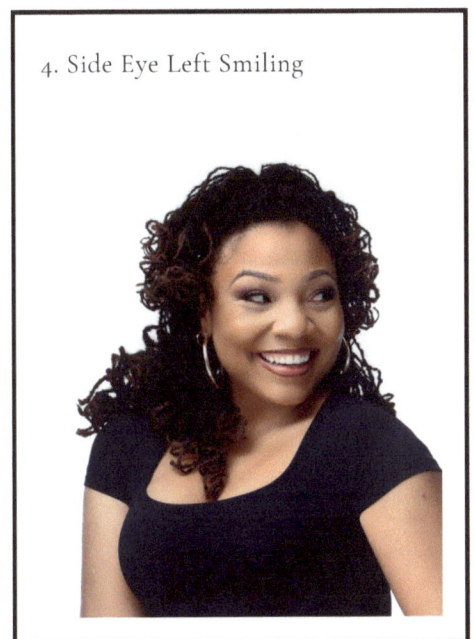

5. Side Eye Right No Smiling

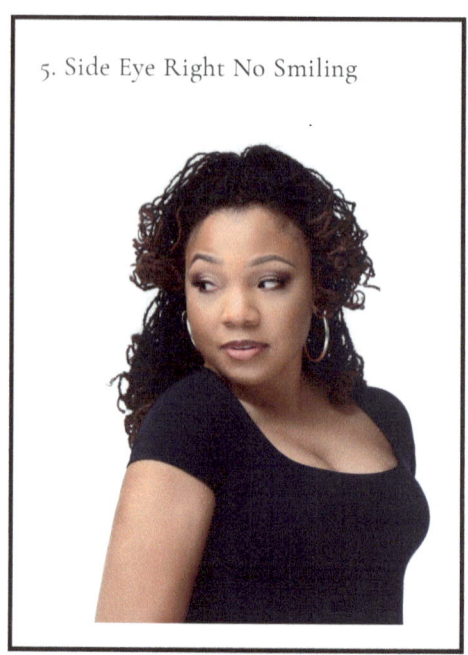

6. Side Eye Right Smiling

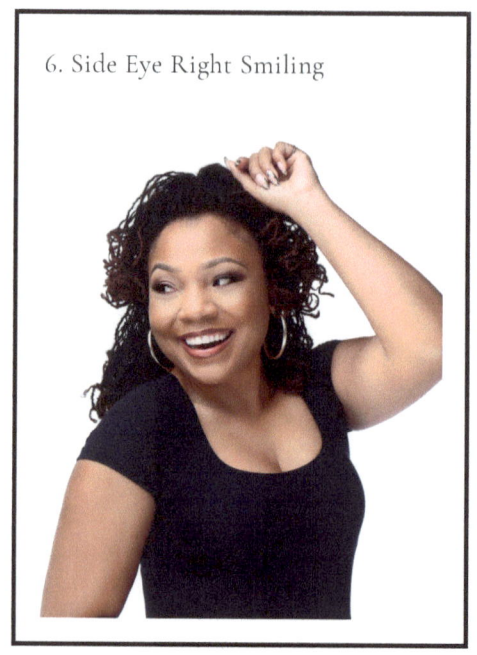

7. Look Up Left No Smile

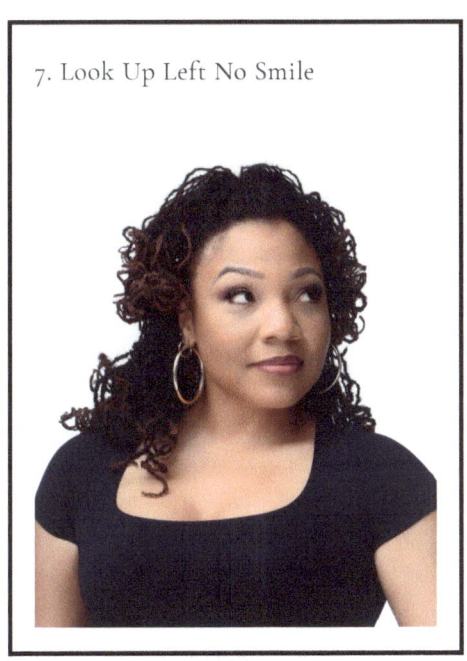

8. Look Up Left Smiling

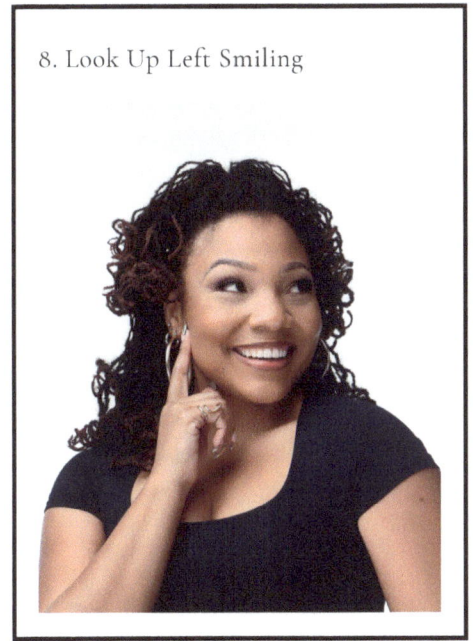

9. Look Up Right No Smile

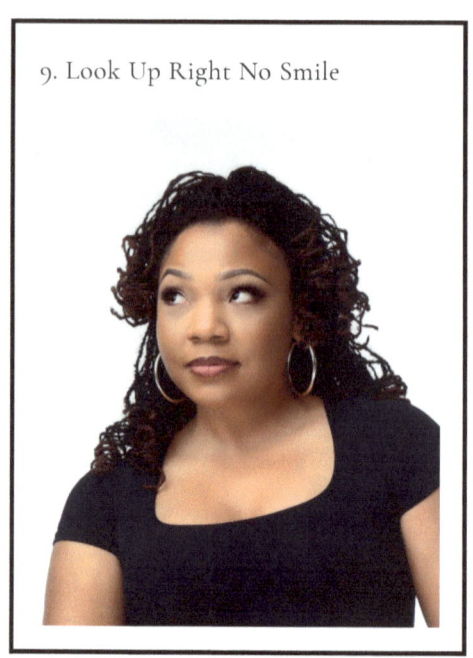

10. Look Up Right Smiling

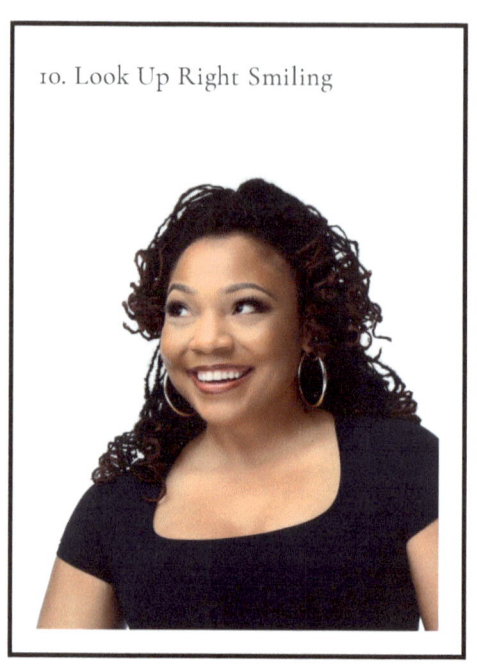

Work The Middle

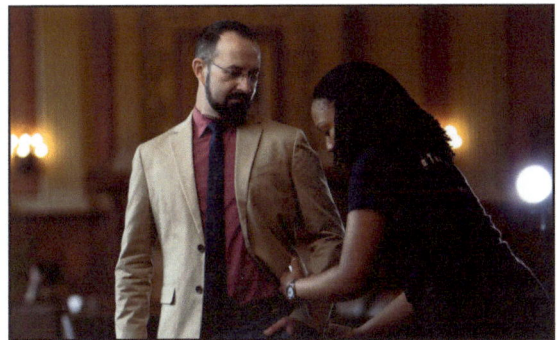

*Half Body shots are typically done for branding photoshoots and special occasions (birthdays, maternity, graduation, etc.). Keep in mind that half body shots can also be used as headshots!

TIP #1 – Wear clothes you are most comfortable and confident in. Dress for your body type, not always what's trending (See *Baby Got Hacks-Dress For Your Body Type, pg. 75*). Doing so will leave you more unsure, fidgety, and insecure about the way you feel in your clothes. Rule of thumb - if you are concerned about your arms, stomach, or legs, DO NOT purchase clothes that magnify that part of your body. Sure, a great photographer can shoot from the most complementary angles and they can also edit your images, but the discouragement in your eyes will tell it all. Remember, photoshoots stem from within and I want you to be confident from start to finish!

TIP #2 – Plan looks at least a month ahead of your photoshoot date. The last thing you want to do is piece outfits together the night before - Yikes! You also want to ensure that everything fits properly and has no holes or tears. This will give you time to return/repurchase things and/or get alterations done.

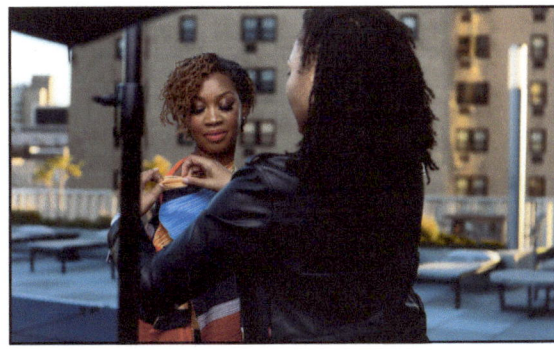

11. Left Hand On Hip

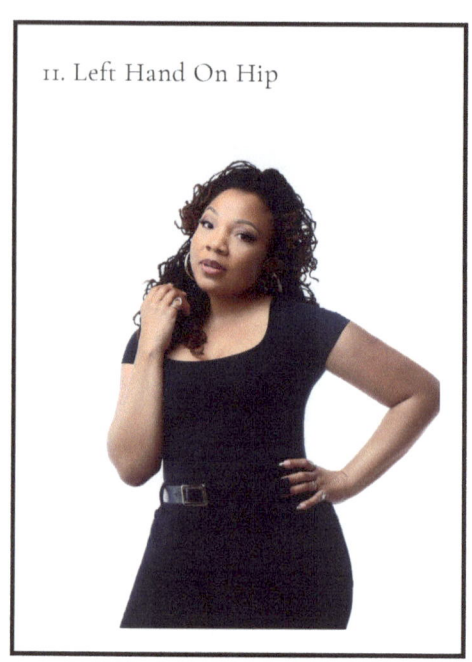

12. Right Hand On Hip

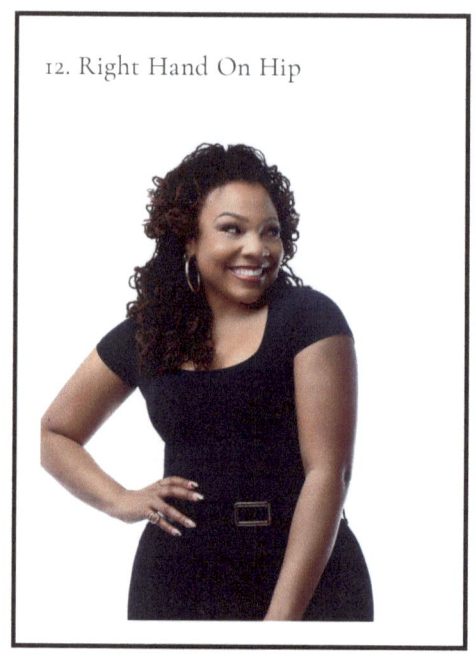

13. Both Hands On Hips (Outward)

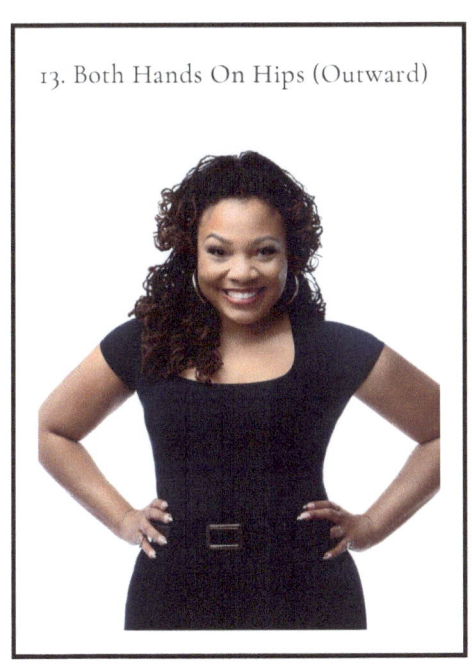

14. Both Hands On Hips (Inward)

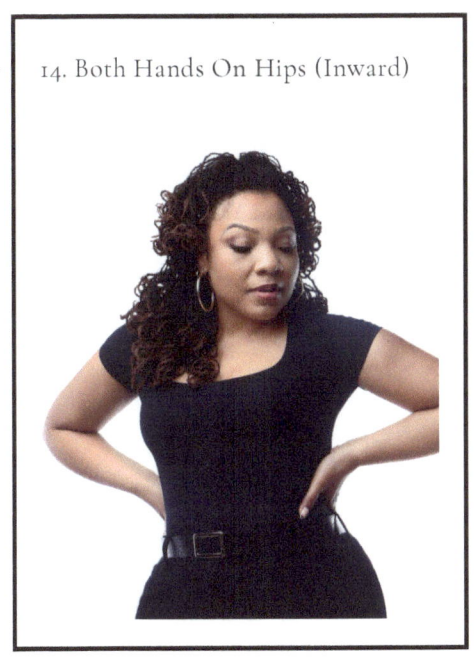

15. Left Hand In Pocket

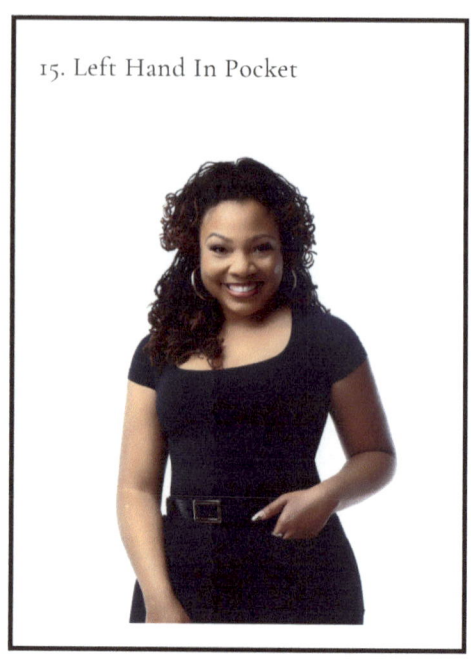

16. Right Hand In Pocket

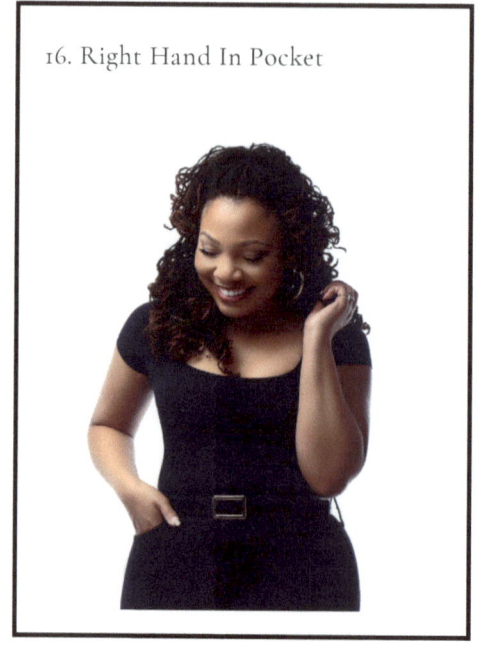

17. Both Hands In Pockets
(4 Fingers In, Thumbs Out)

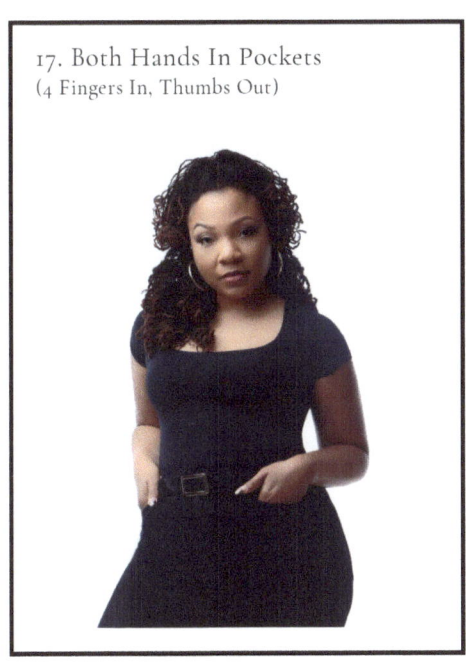

18. Belt Loops
(Hook Your Thumbs, 4 Fingers Relaxed)

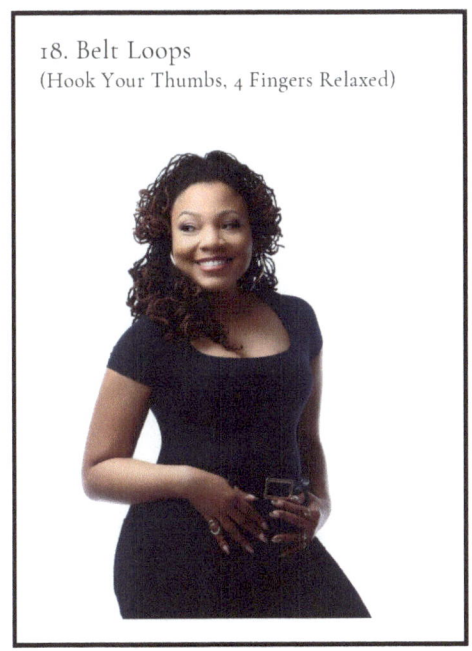

19. Double Arm Fold
(Straight On)

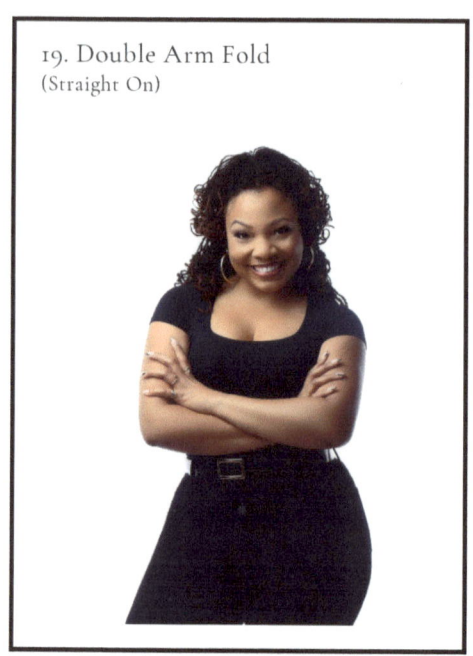

20. Double Arm Fold
(Towards Light Source)

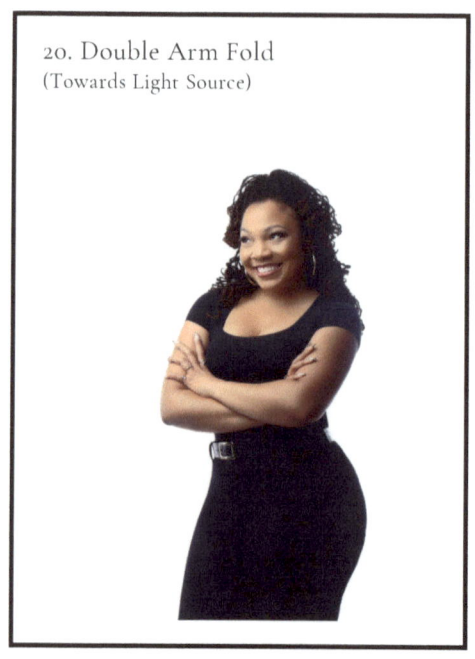

21. Double Arm Fold
(Side Eye To The Left)

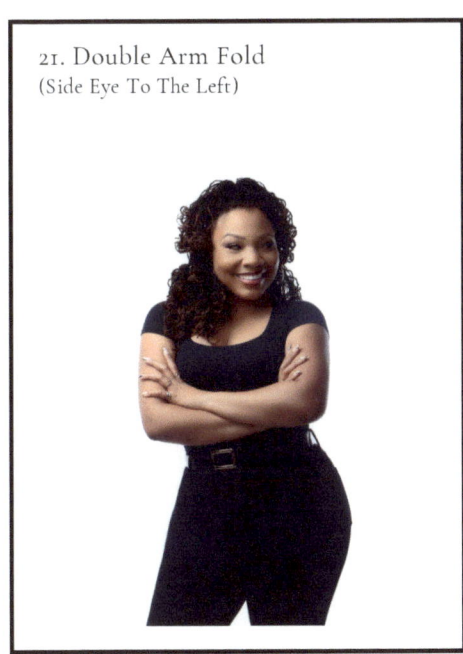

22. Double Arm Fold
(Side Eye To The Right)

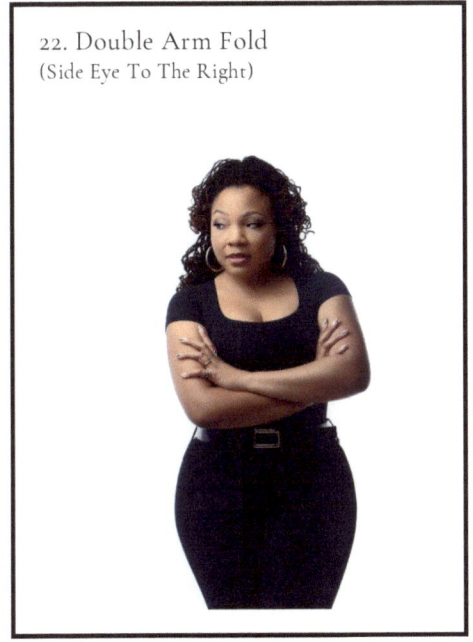

23. Half Arm Fold
(Hand Up)

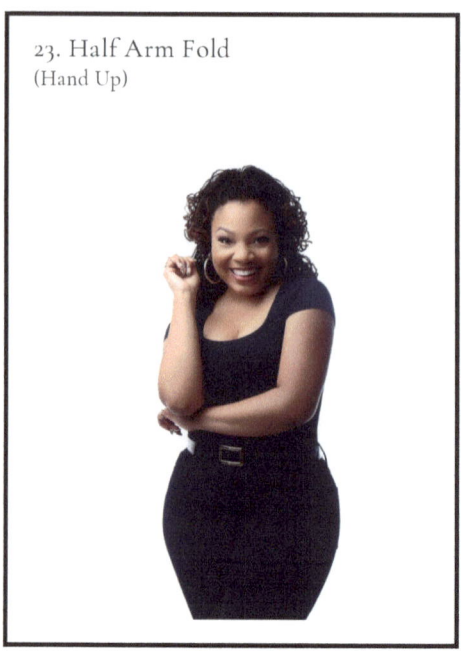

24. Half Arm Fold
(Index Finger On Cheek)

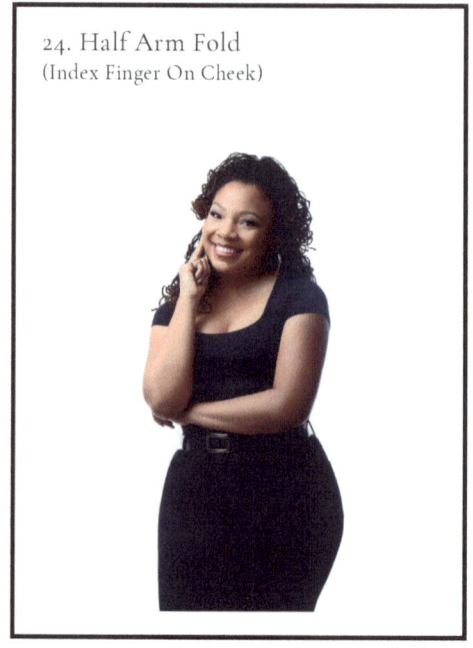

25. Half Arm Fold
(Hand Under Chin)

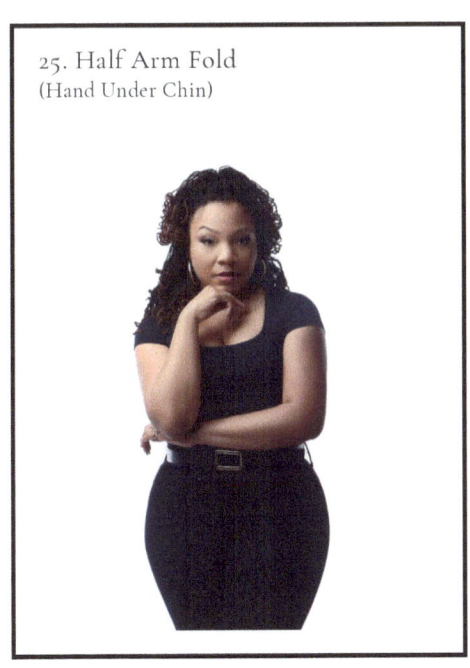

26. Half Arm Fold
(Hand In Hair)

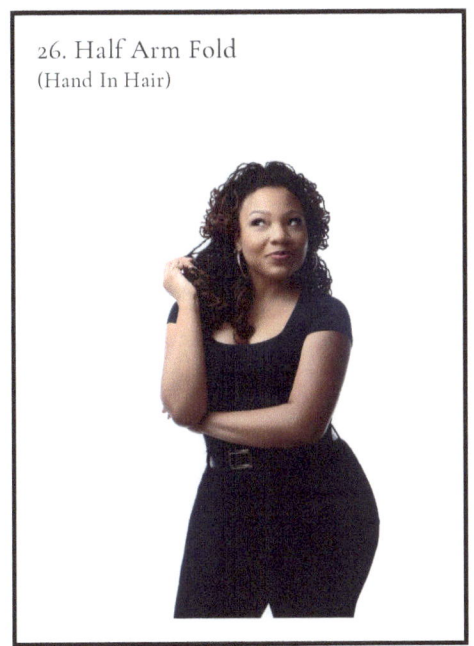

27. Half Arm Fold
(Hand Behind Ear)

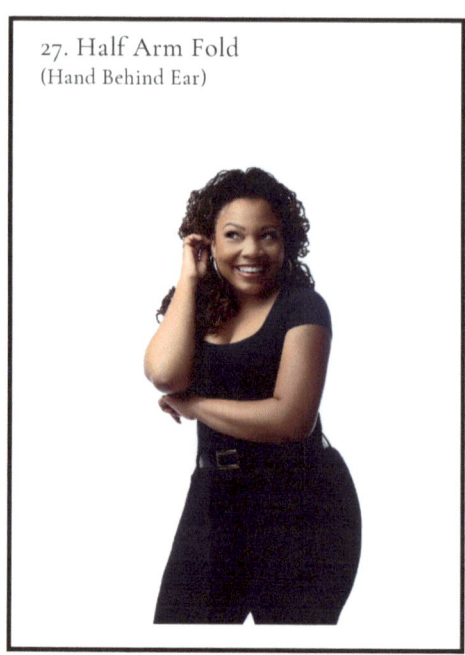

28. Half Arm Fold
(Hand Behind Ear, Look Down)

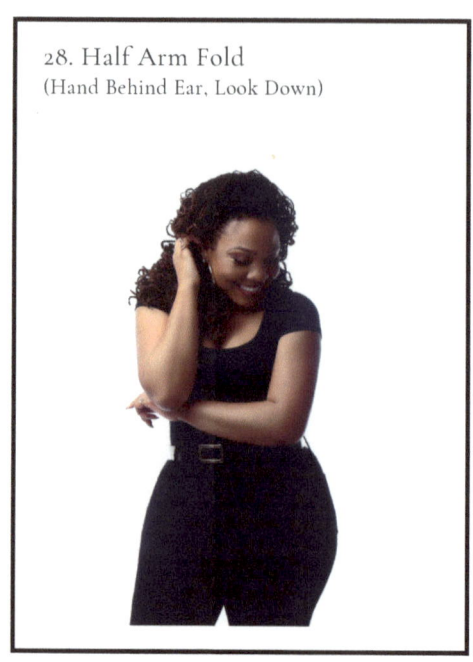

29. Half Arm Fold
(Look Straight, Hand on Shoulder)

30. Half Arm Fold
(Look Up, Hand on Shoulder)

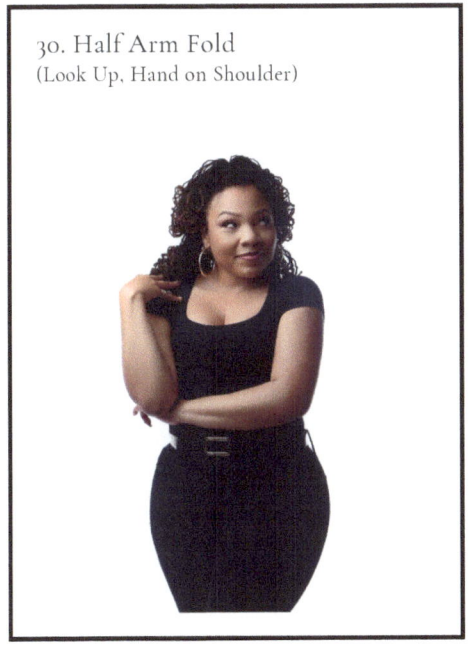

31. Half Arm Fold
(Chin In Shoulder, Look Straight)

32. Half Arm Fold
(Chin In Shoulder, Eyes Closed)

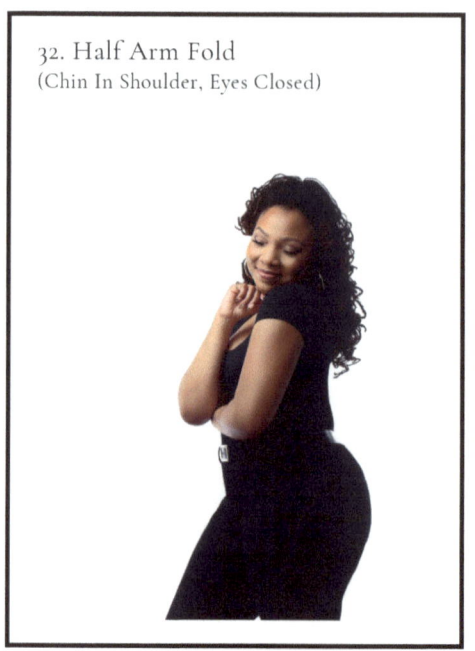

33. Look Over Shoulder

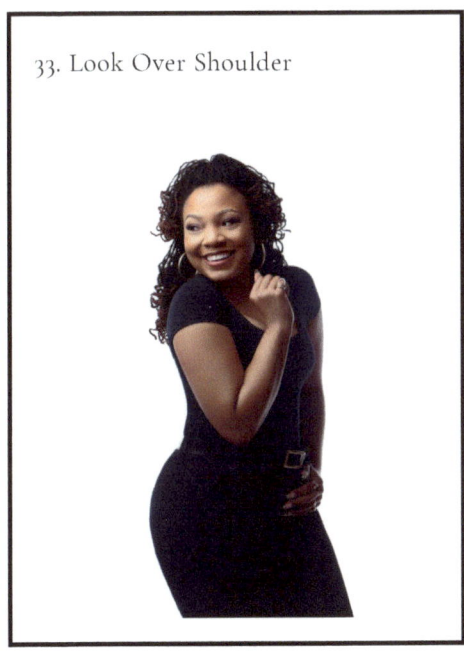

34. Look Over Shoulder, Look Up

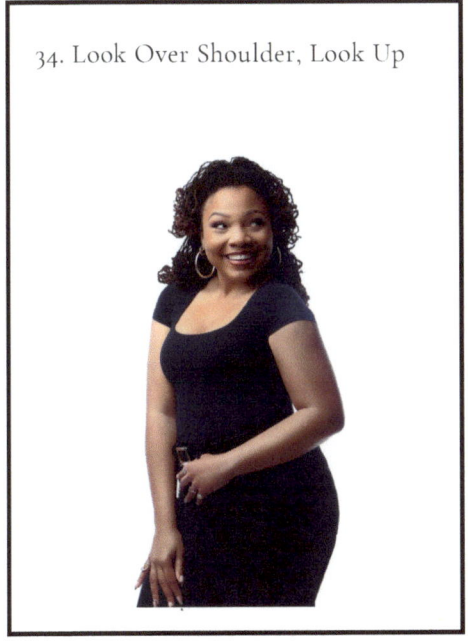

35. Look Down, Smile

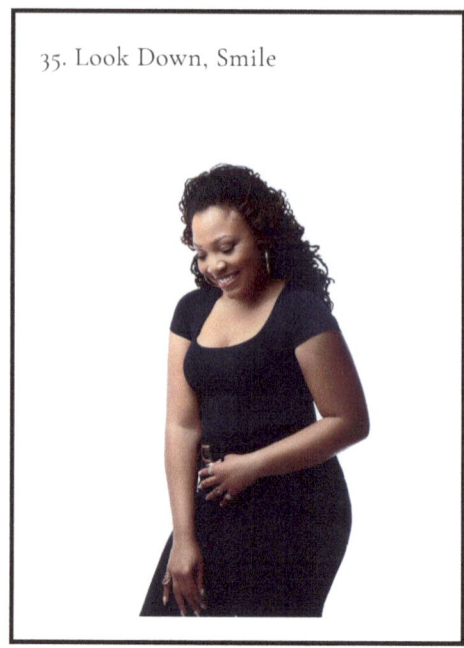

36. One Hand On Neck, One Hand On Head, Look Straight

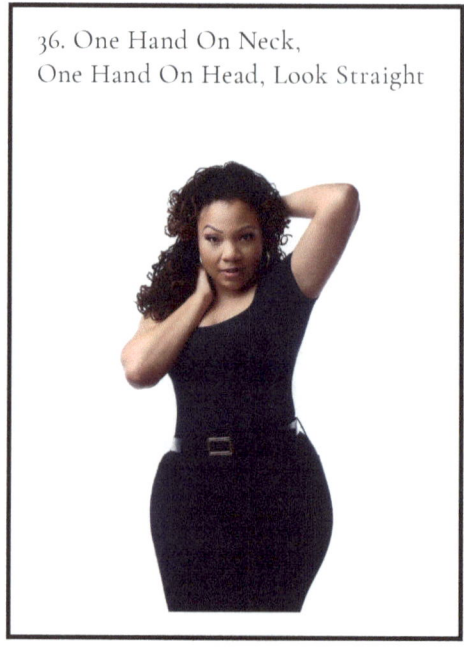

37. One Hand On Neck,
One Hand On Head, Look Up

38. One Hand On Neck,
One Hand On Head, Eyes Closed

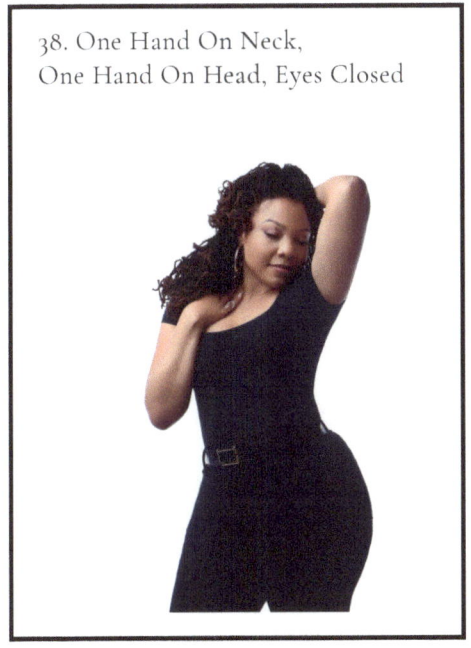

39. Look Straight On, Half Hug

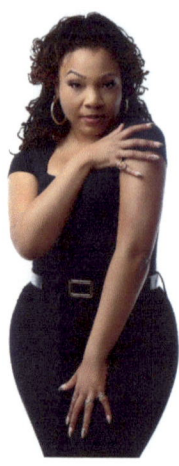

40. Look Straight Smiling, Half Hug

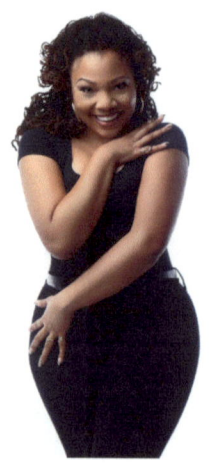

41. Look Straight On, Whole Hug

42. Eyes Closed, Whole Hug

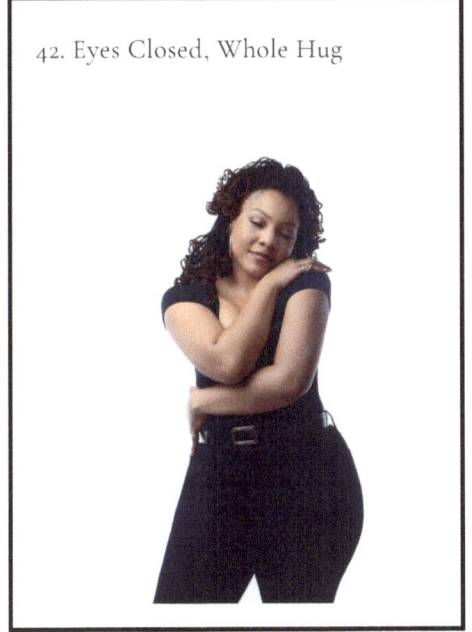

43. Eyes Closed, Whole Hug, Head In Hand

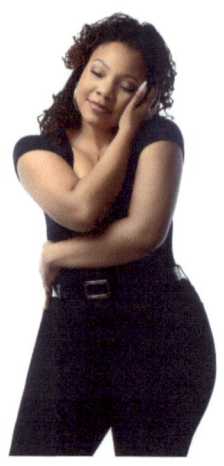

44. Point w/Thumb, Look Over Shoulder

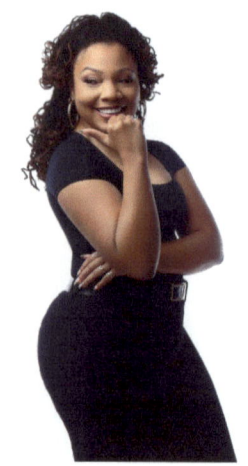

45. Point w/Index Fingers
To The Side

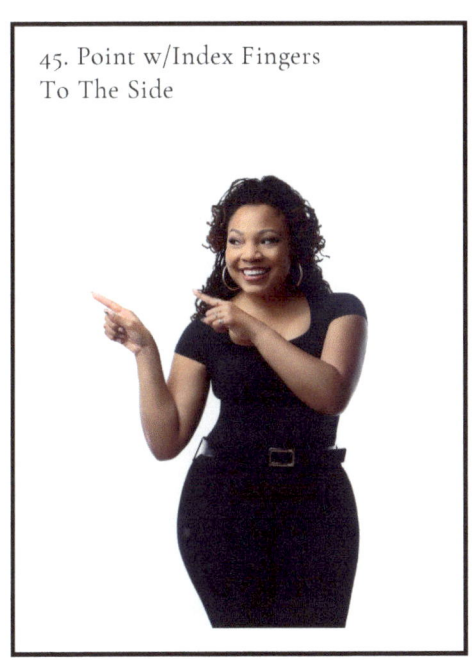

46. Point w/Index Fingers
Pointed Up

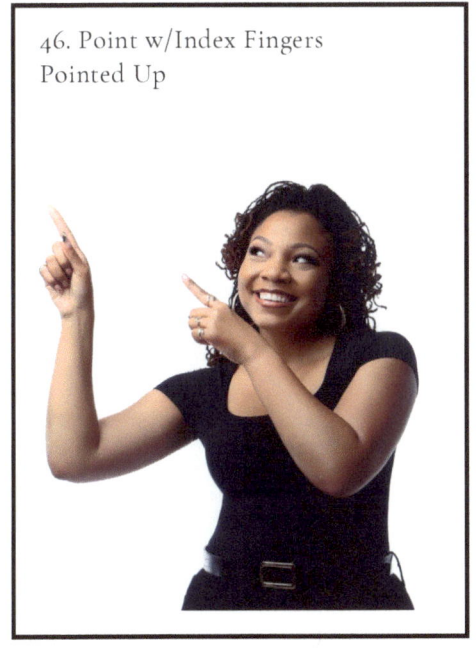

47. Point w/Index Fingers Above Head

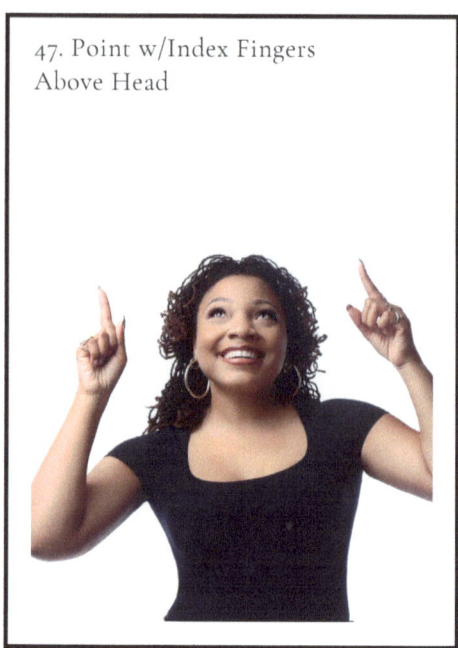

48. One Hand Out Flat

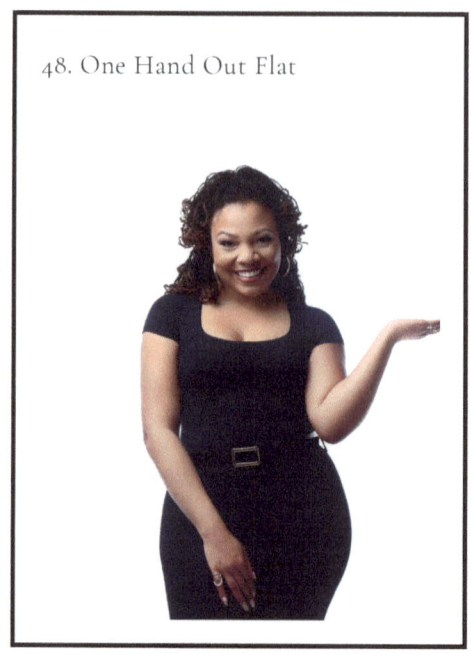

49. Both Hands Out Flat

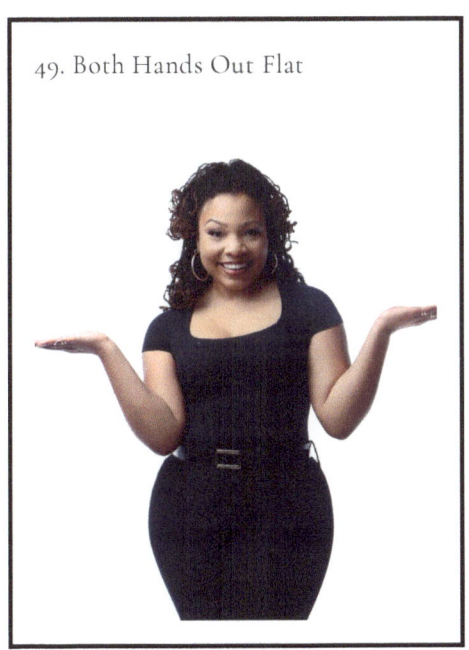

Get Me
Bodied

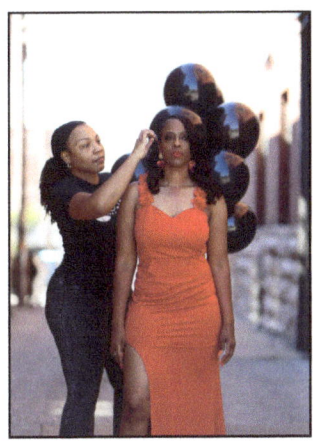

*Full Body shots are generally a continuation from half body shots. You honestly can't have one without the other.

TIP #1 – (I repeat!) Make sure everything is clean and ironed. Editing out stains and wrinkles will cost you a pretty penny.

TIP #2 – Try to wear shoes that are at least semi-comfortable. I totally understand that shoes sometimes make the outfit, but it can also break your energy and facial expressions if your feet are hurting. Also, practice walking in them at home as much as possible. You never know what creative things your photographer may have up their sleeve! Stay ready, hunty!

TIP #3 – The 'triangle' method will be your best friend! Bend those knees, arms, and elbows! It's an absolute guarantee that I will incorporate this into each photoshoot I do. By simply separating your limbs from your body, you will create depth, symmetry, and curves. It will make you look and feel better in your clothes while showing personality (See *Baby Got Hacks-Degrees Of Separation, pg. 77*).

TIP #4 – Don't limit yourself to standing - have fun with it!

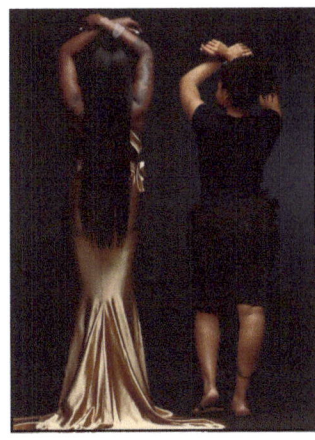

50. One Arm Down, Other Hand Up/In Hair, Legs Separated, Knee Bent, Toes Pointed

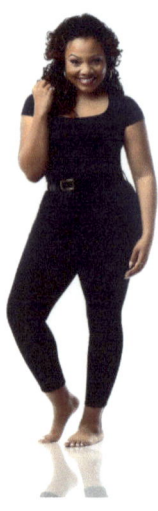

51. Half Arm Fold, Legs Separated, Knee Bent, Toes Pointed

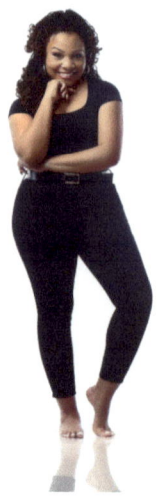

52. Half Arm Fold, Foot Crossover

53. Double Arm Fold, Legs Separated, Knee Bent, Toes Pointed

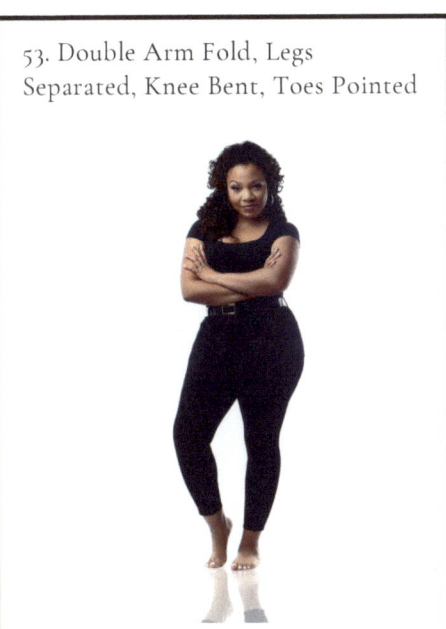

54. Half Arm Fold,
Leg Cross Over

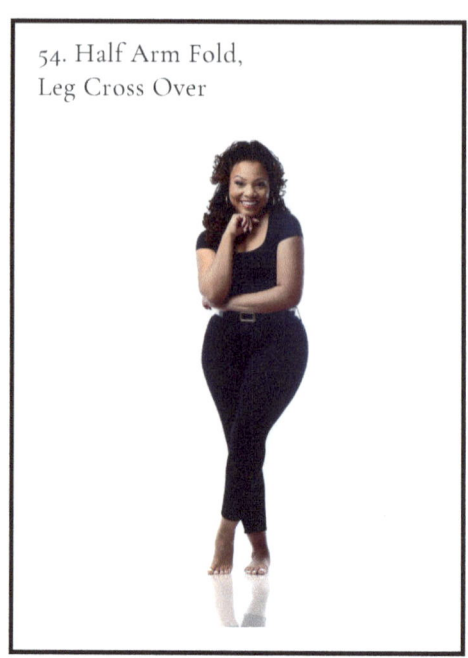

55. Double Arm Fold,
Foot Cross Over

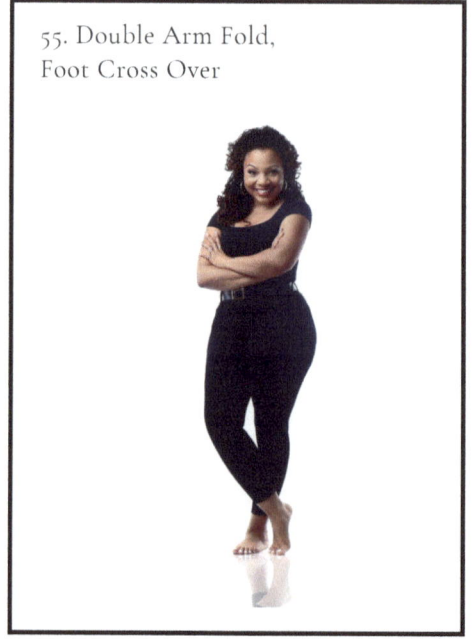

56. One Hand In Pocket/On Hip, Foot Cross Over

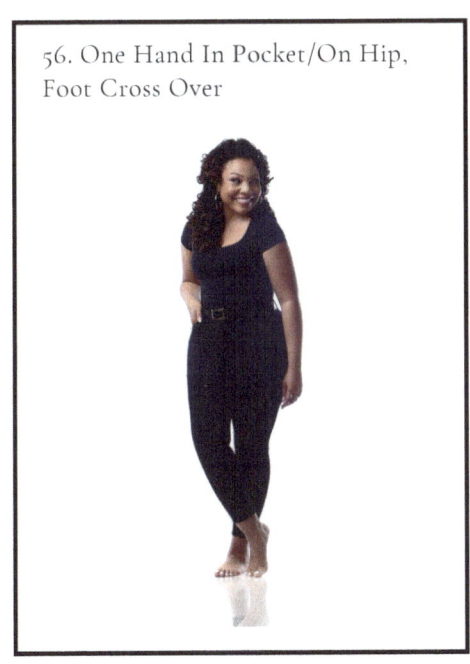

57. Both Hands In Pockets/On Hips, Leg Cross Over

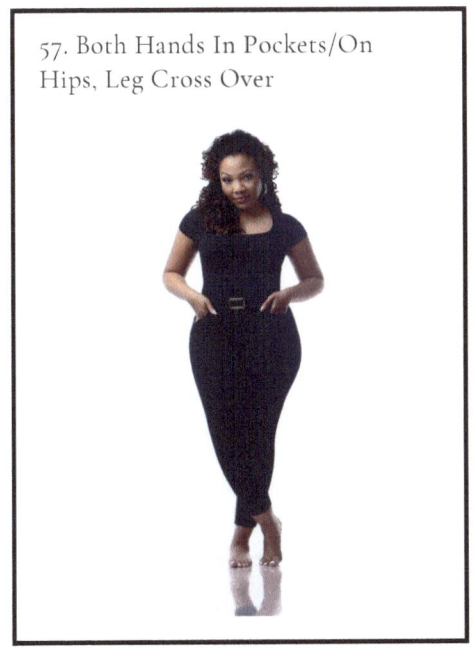

58. One Hand On Hip, Hand On Top Of Head, Legs Separated

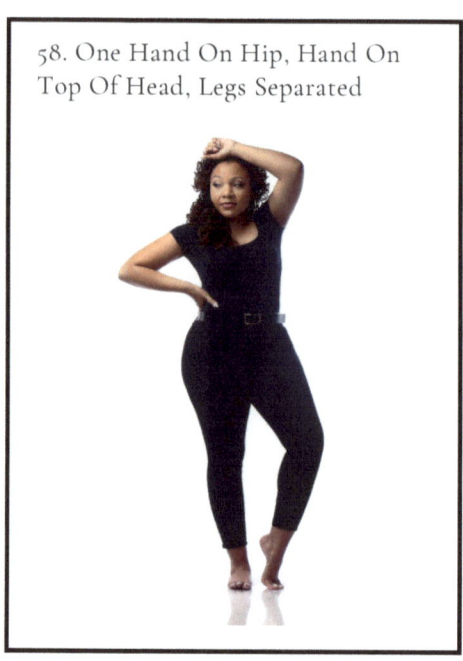

59. One Hand On Hip, Hand On Top Of Head, Legs Separated, Turned 45 Degrees

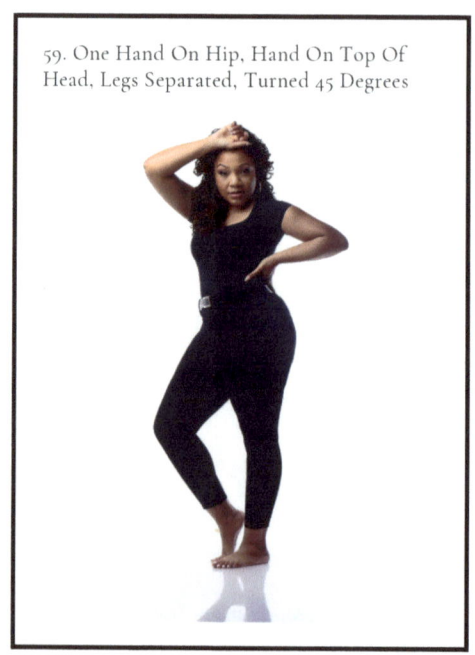

60. One Hand On Hip, Hand On Top Of Head, Legs Close Together, One Foot Pointed

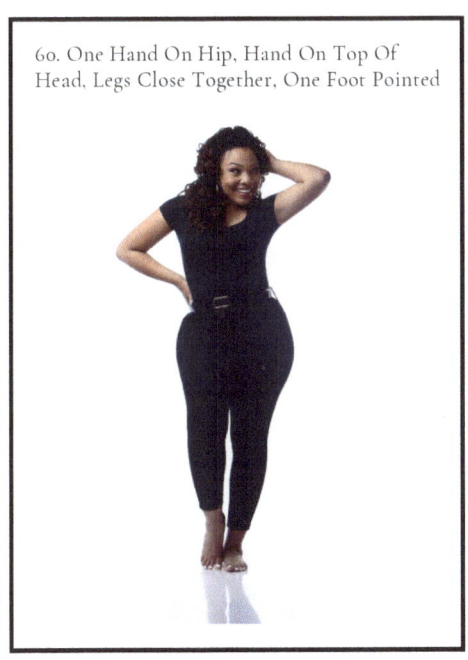

61. One Hand On Hip, Hand On Top Of Head, Legs Separated, One Foot Pointed (Straight On)

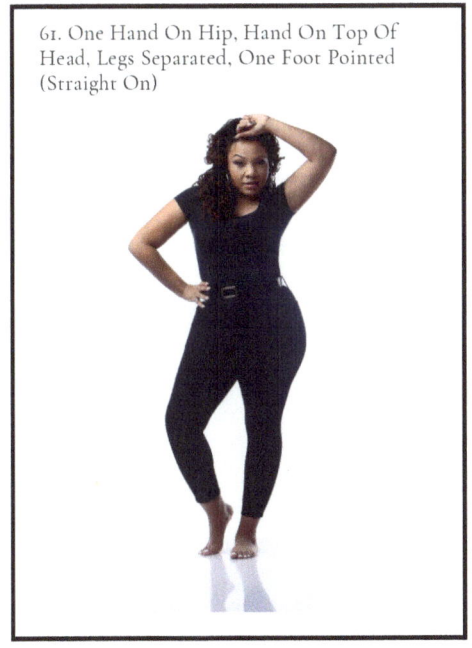

62. Both Hands On Hips, Legs Close Together, One Foot Pointed, Look Straight

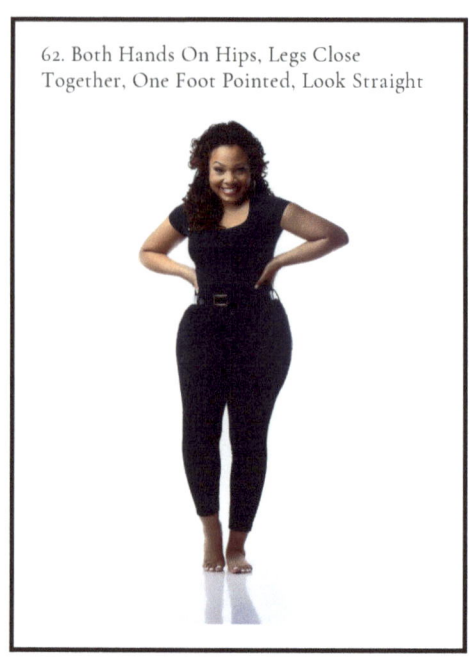

63. Both Hands On Hips, Legs Close Together, One Foot Pointed, Look Away

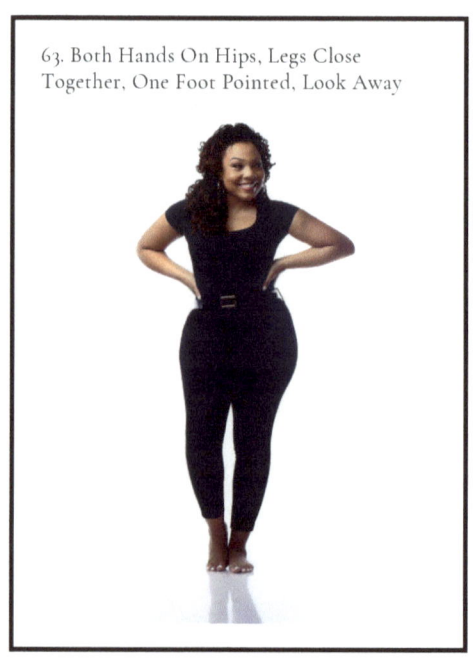

64. Both Hands On Hips, Legs Close Together, One Foot Pointed, Look Up

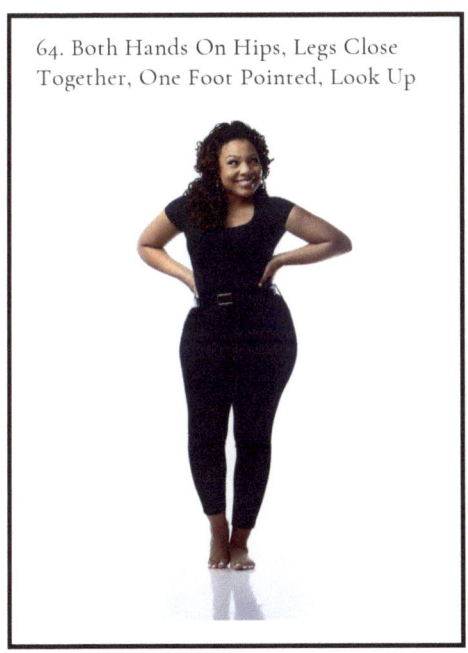

Sittin'
On Top
Of The
World

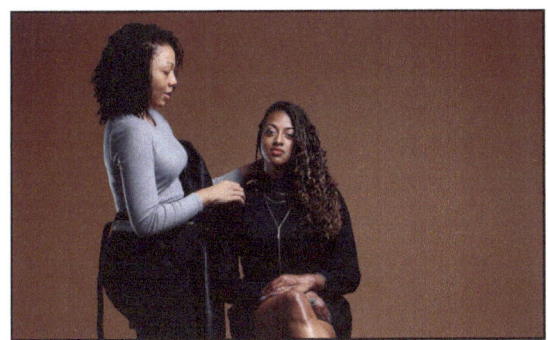

TIP #1 – Always consider your posture. Most times you will be straight and astute, unless you are channeling something fresh out of an editorial magazine.

TIP #2 – Sitting back in some chairs can leave you looking too relaxed and even wider than you would like. Try sitting up and on the edge of the seat (chair or couch). You are forced to have better posture which will elongate your neck and back. This also gives you a chance to play around with feet and arm pose options!

TIP #3 – Having a chair or stool handy doesn't always mean you have to sit in them. You could stand beside them or sit with your back against them - get creative!

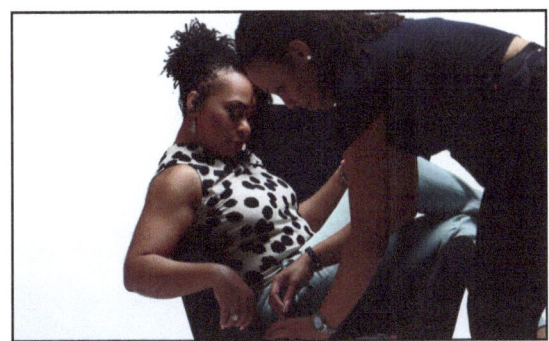

65. Side Ankle Cross, Look Straight

Chair

66. Side Ankle Cross, Look Away

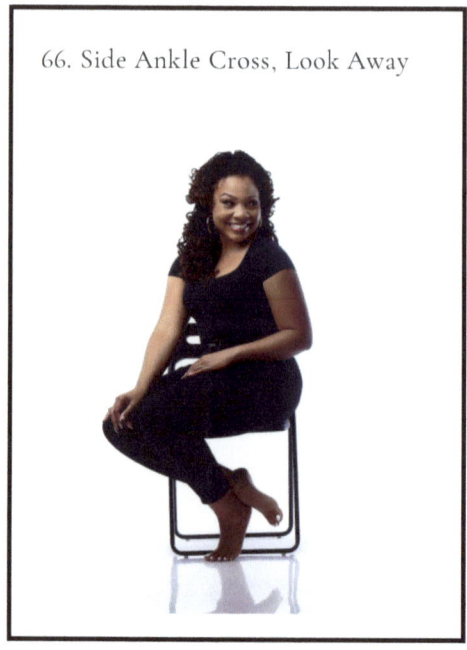

67. Knee Cross

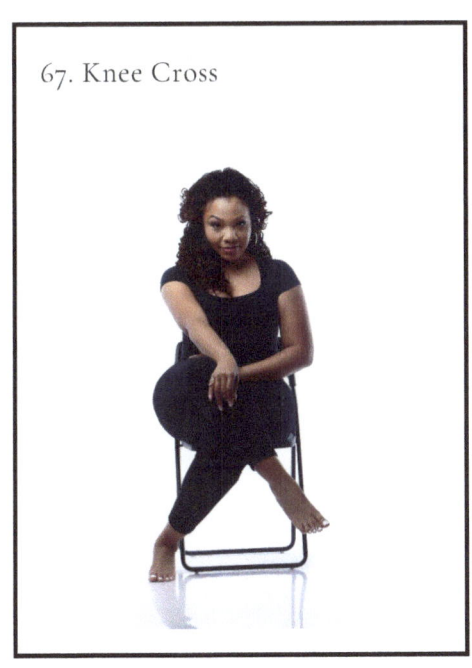

68. Knee Cross, Hand Under Chin

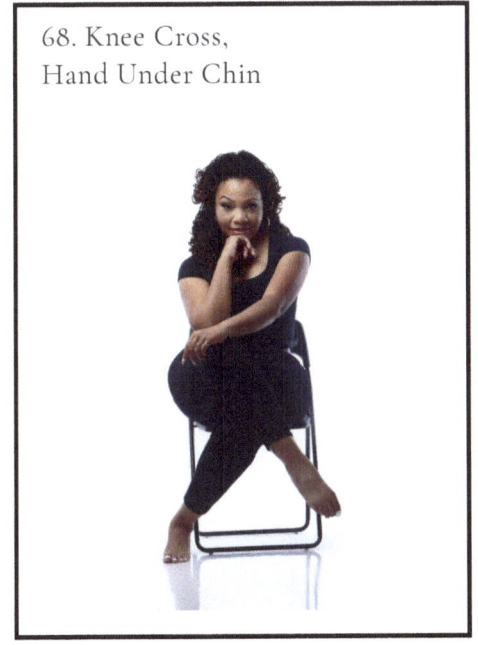

69. Leg Part Lean

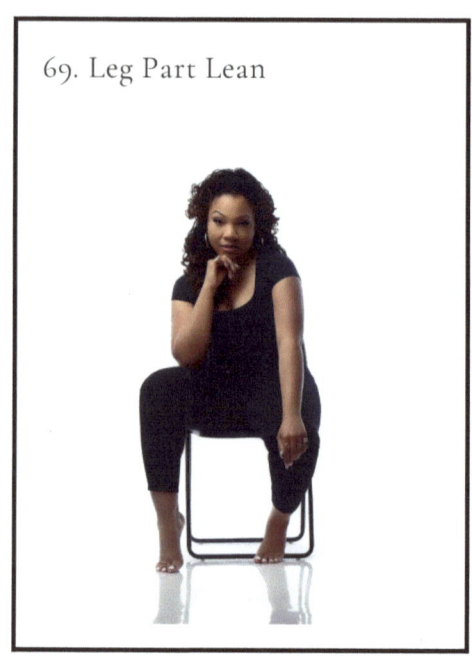

70. Sexy Slouch

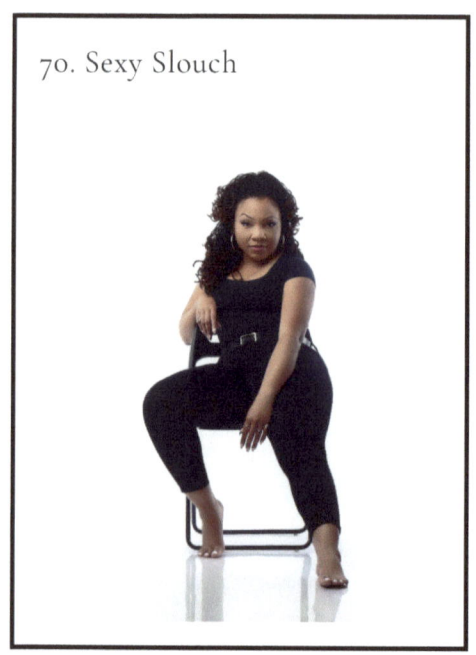

71. Sideways Knee Cross

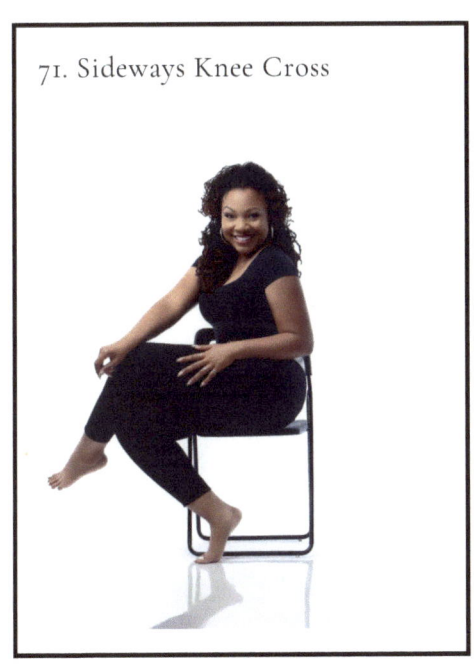

72. Part Legs, Lean In Straight On

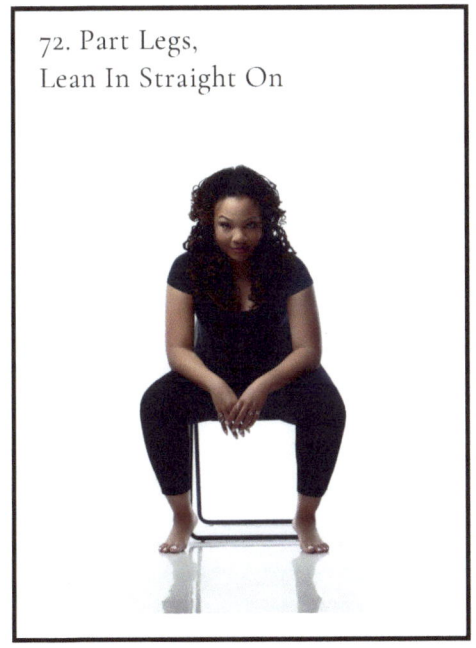

73. Part Legs, Lean To The Right

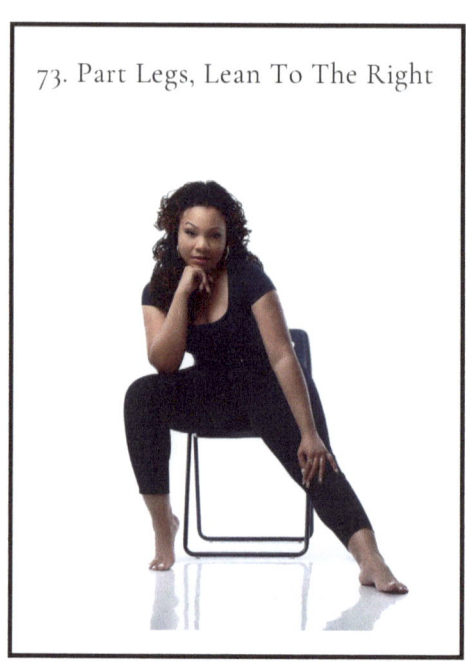

74. Part Legs, Lean To The Left

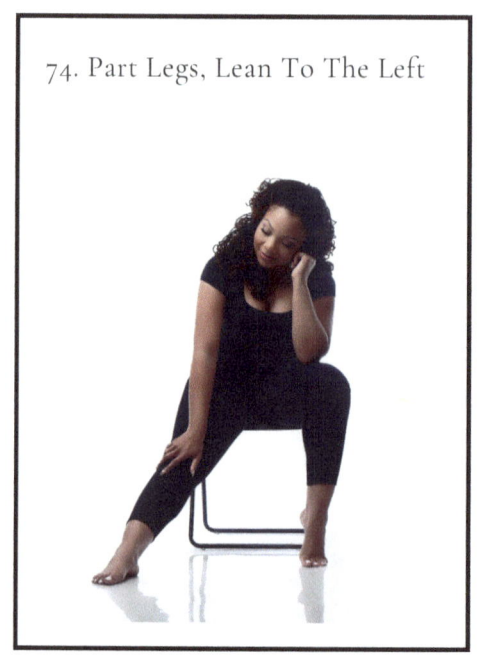

75. Sideways, Legs Separated, Knees Bent

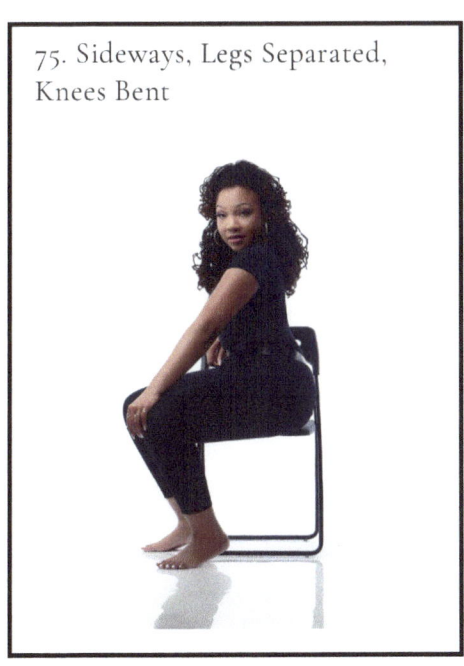

76. Sideways, Legs Separated, Knees Bent, Lean Forward

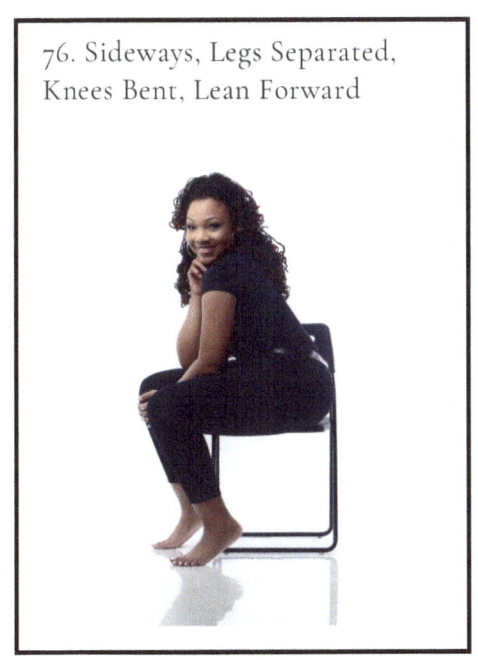

77. Chair Straddle

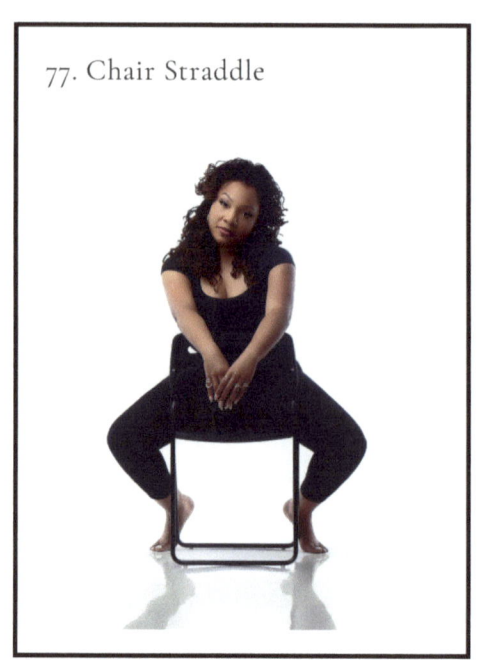

78. Chair Straddle, Arm On Back Of Chair

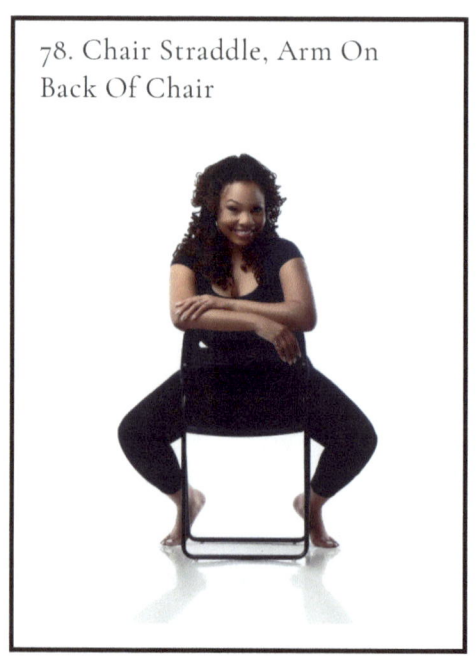

79. Chair Straddle Sideways

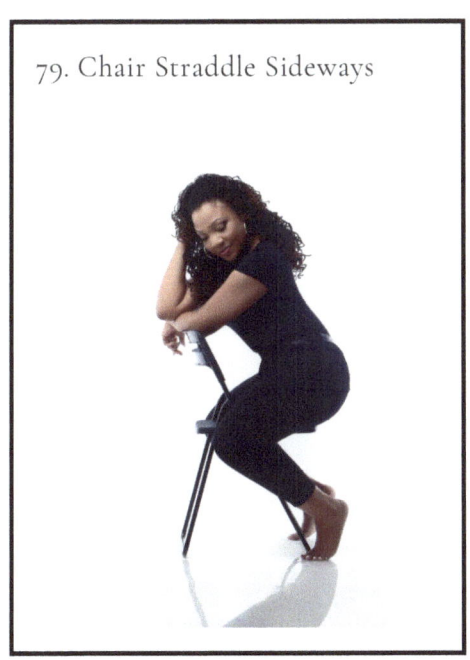

80. One Foot On Stool, One Foot On Floor, Hand(s) On Thigh(s)

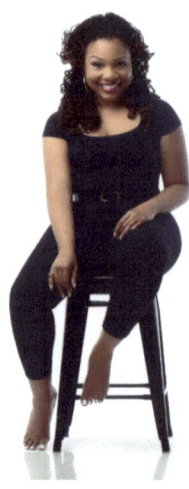

Stool

81. One Foot On Stool, One Foot On Floor, One Hand On Thigh, One Hand On Stool

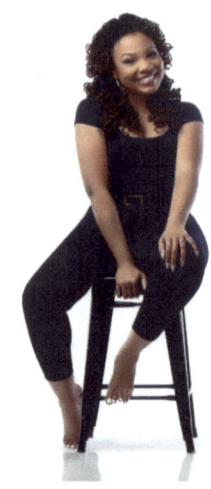

82. One Foot On Stool, One Foot On Floor, Hand Under Chin, Leaning

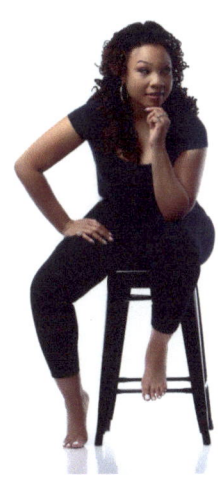

83. Sideways, One Foot On Stool, One Foot On Floor, Both Hands On Stool

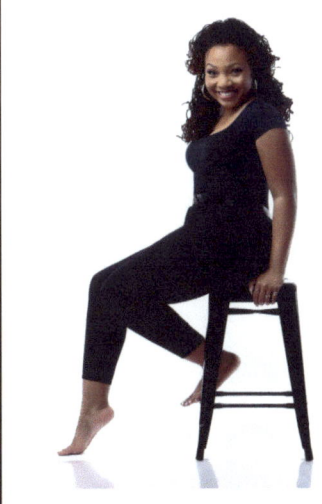

84. Sideways, One Foot On Stool, One Foot On Floor, Hand On Stool, Hand On Head

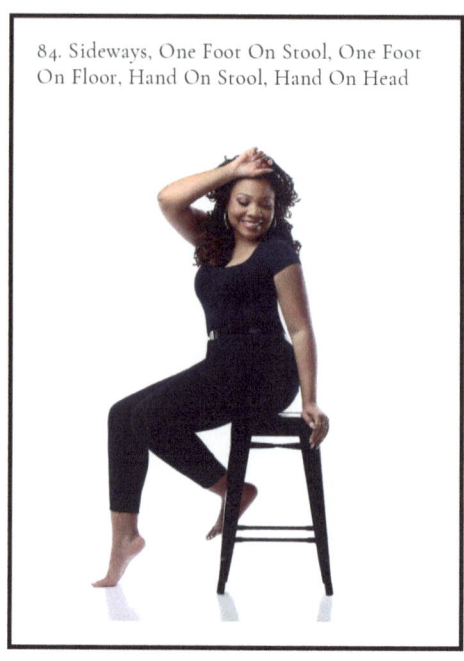

85. Sitting On The Floor, Beside The Stool

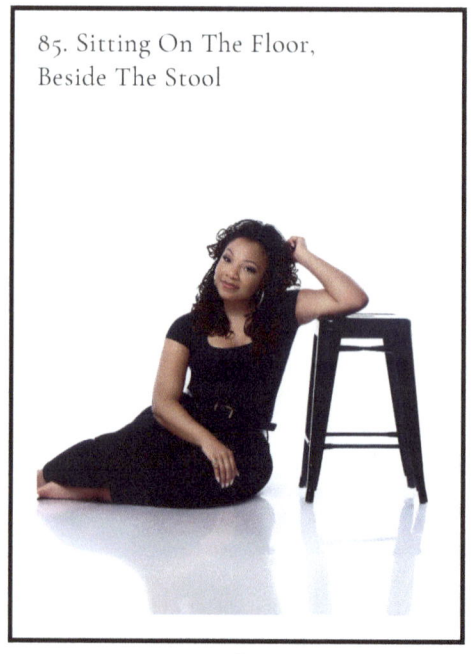

86. Kneeling, Looking Forward

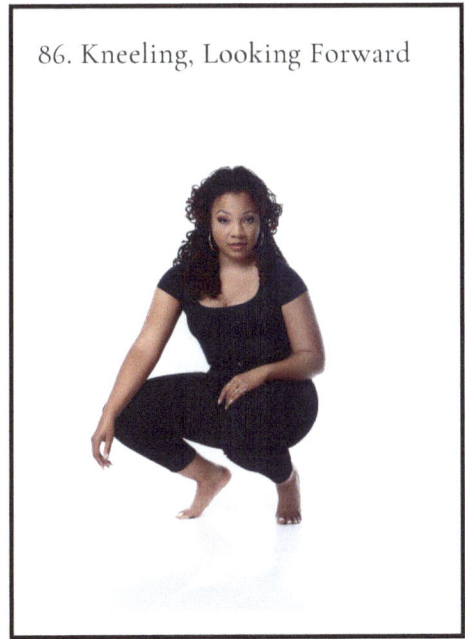

Floor

87. Kneeling, Looking Away

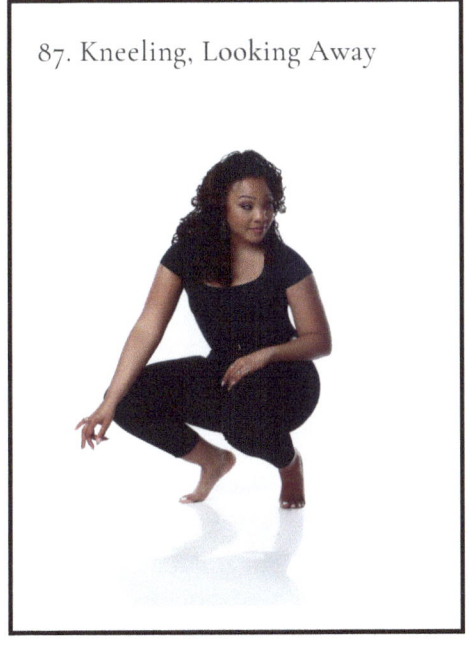

88. Sitting, Leg Cross, Hand Under Chin

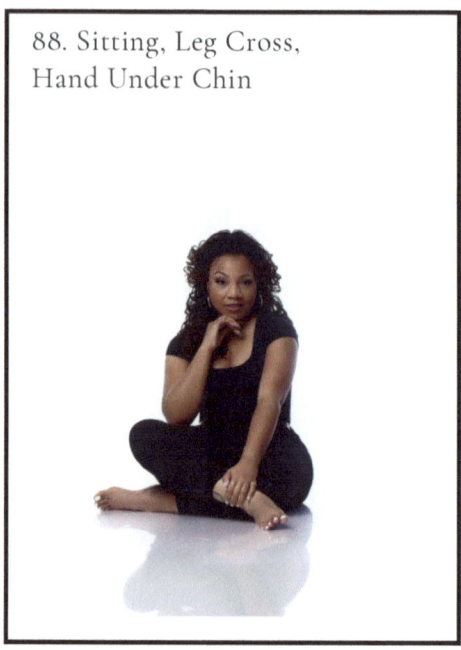

89. Sitting, Leg Cross, Both Hands On Front Leg

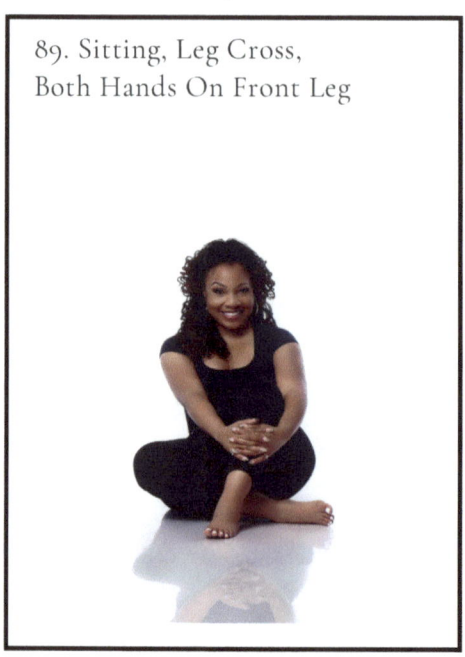

90. Sitting, Leg Cross, Both Hands On The Floor

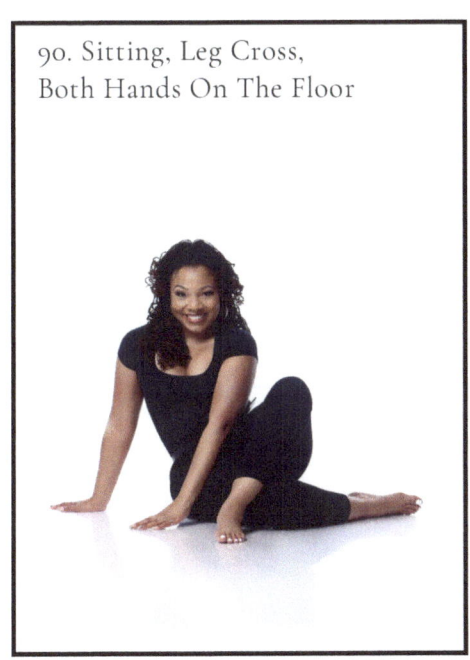

91. Sitting, Leg Cross, One Hand On Knee, One Hand On Floor

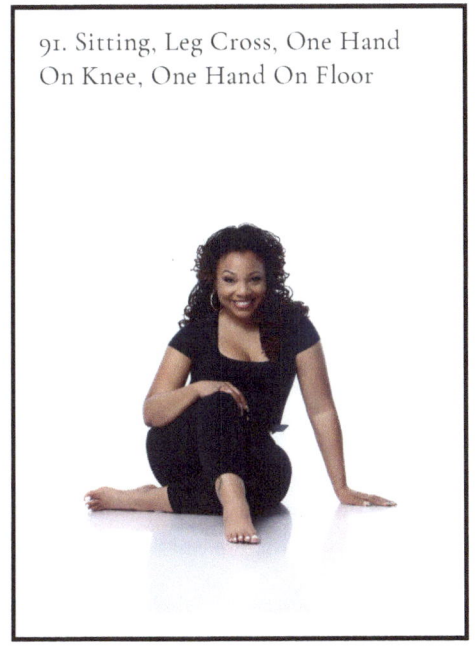

92. Sitting On Hip

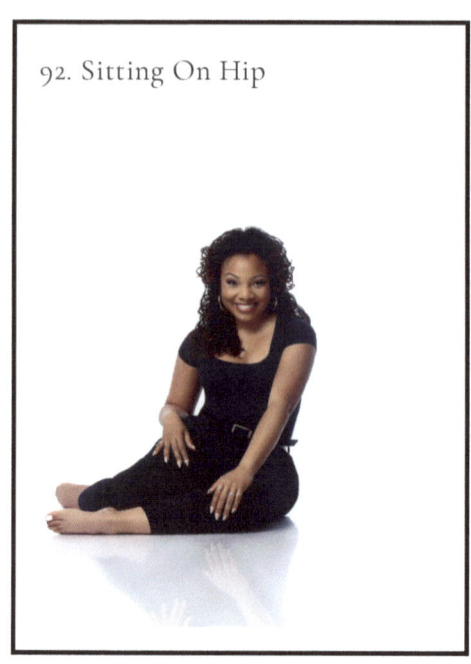

93. On Hip, Leg Cross, Hand On Face, Elbow On Knee

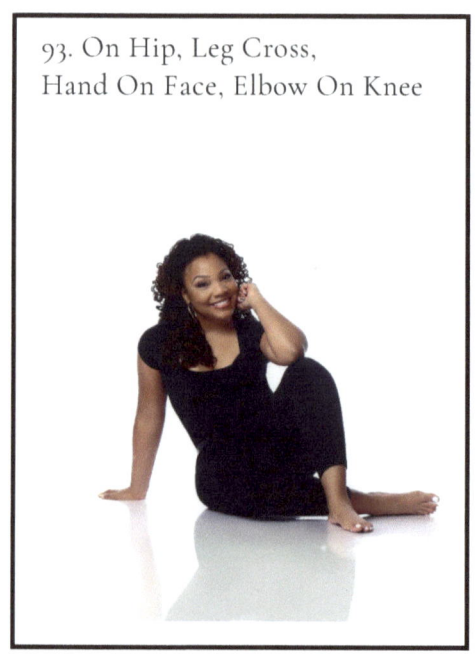

94. On Hip, Leg Cross, Hand Under Chin, Elbow On Knee

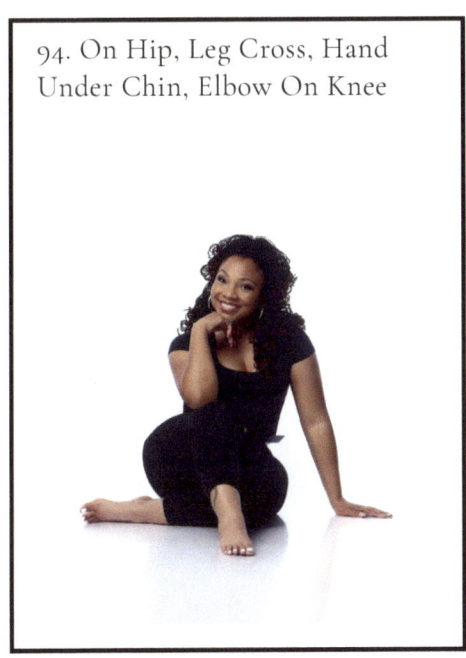

95. On Hip, Legs Staggered, Hand On Knee, Opposite Hand On Shoulder

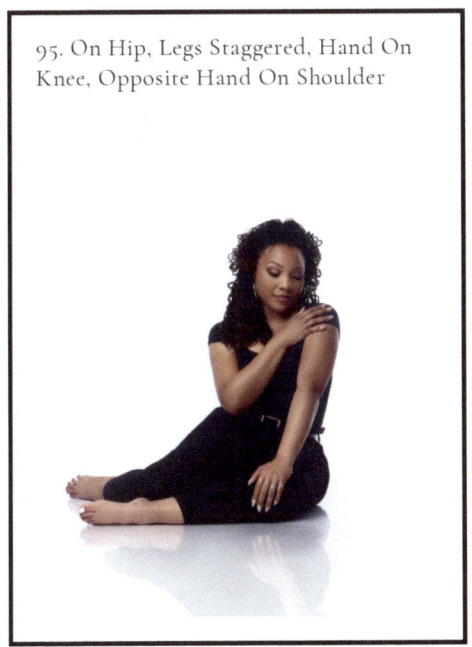

Prop It Like It's *Hot*

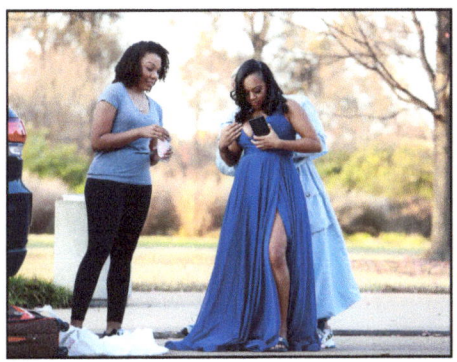

TIP #1 – Props are actually anything extra that you bring to the set. Other prop examples: a laptop, a coffee mug, a microphone, flowers, a hat, and even products you sell! The sky is limitless!

TIP #2 – Ask your photographer if they have props available to use. If so, ask if they can send you pictures or if you can stop by their studio to see what they have. This would be a great way to save some time and money!

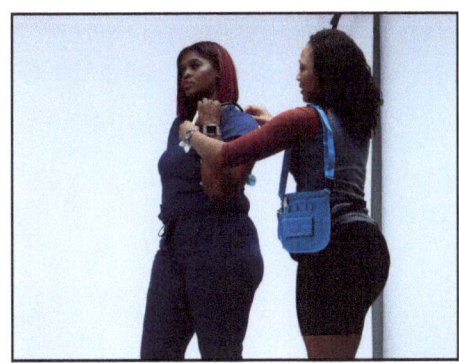

Coat/Jacket

96. Hands In Front

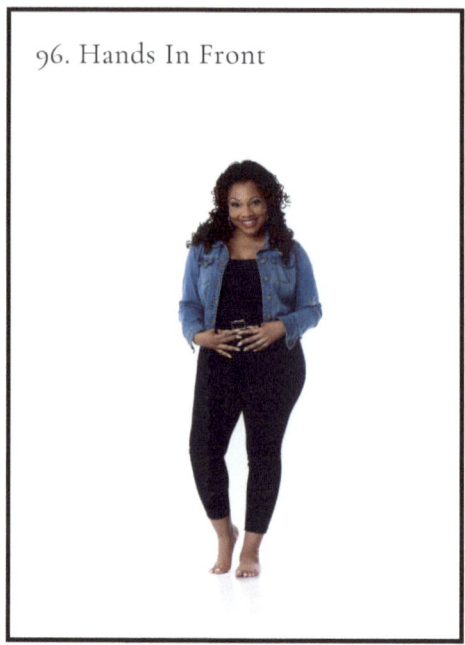

97. Hand In One Pocket

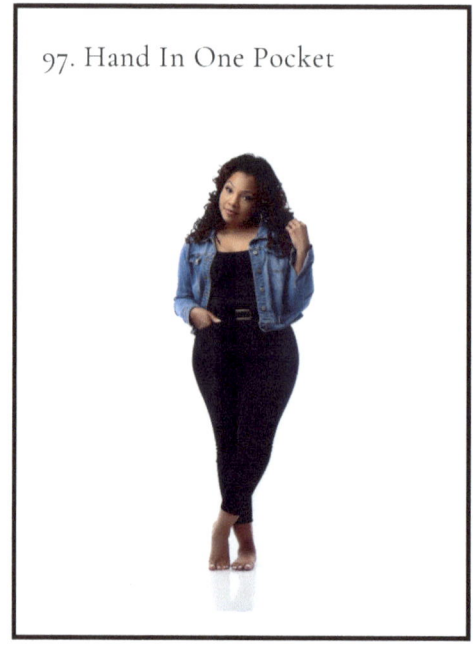

98. Hands In Both Pockets

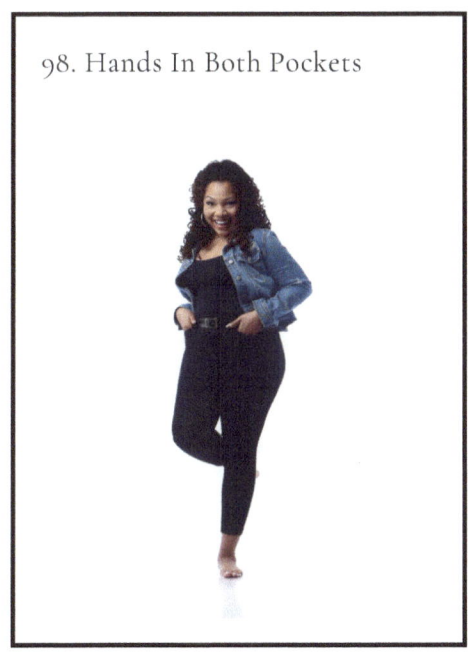

99. One Hand On Lapel, One Hand In Pocket, Look Over Shoulder

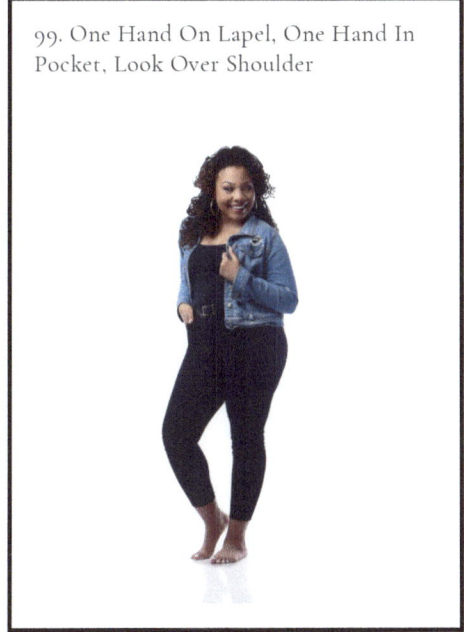

100. Draped Over Both Shoulders

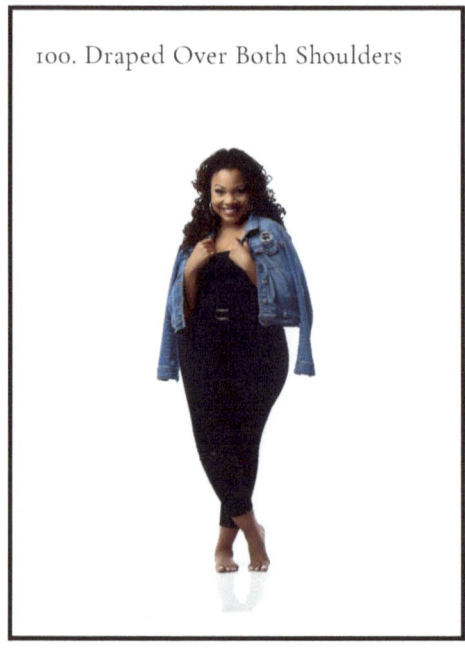

101. Draped Over One Shoulder

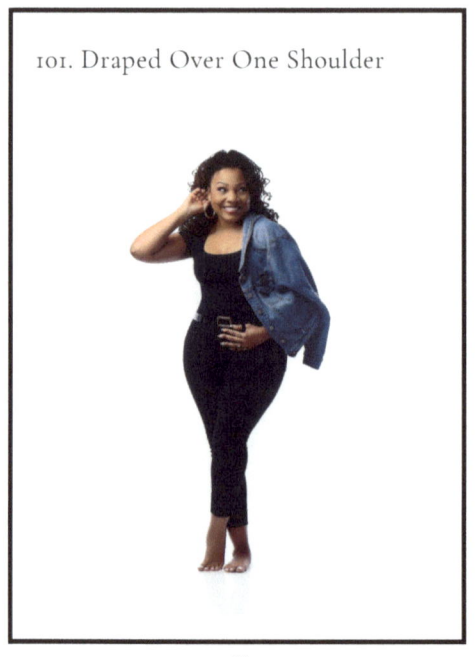

102. Thrown Over One Shoulder

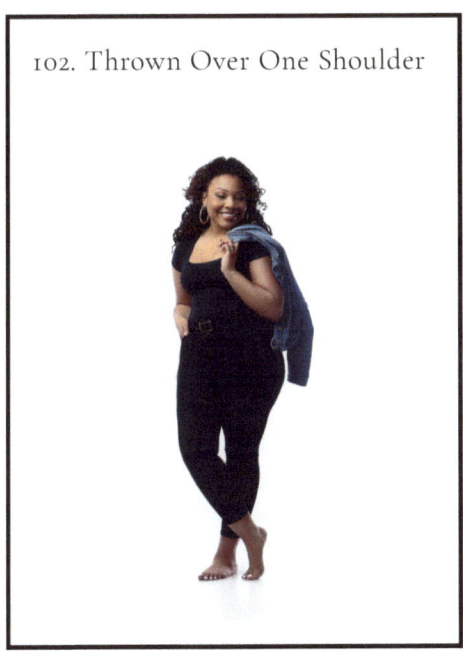

103. Casually Holding

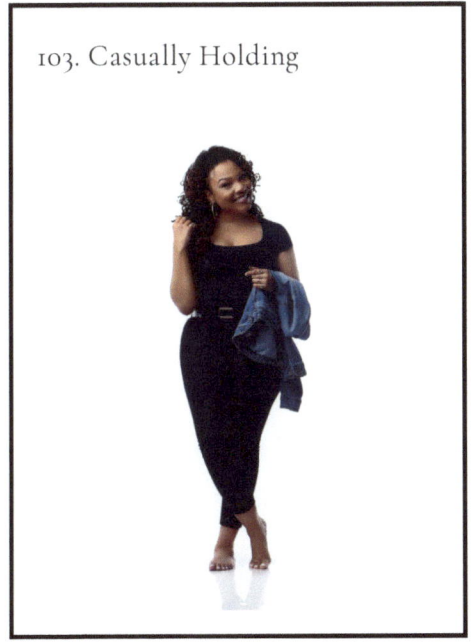

104. Two Hand Hold In Front

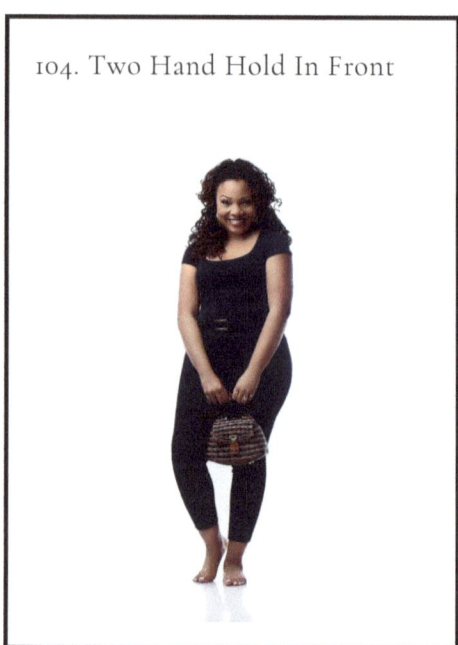

Purse

105. One Hand Side Hold

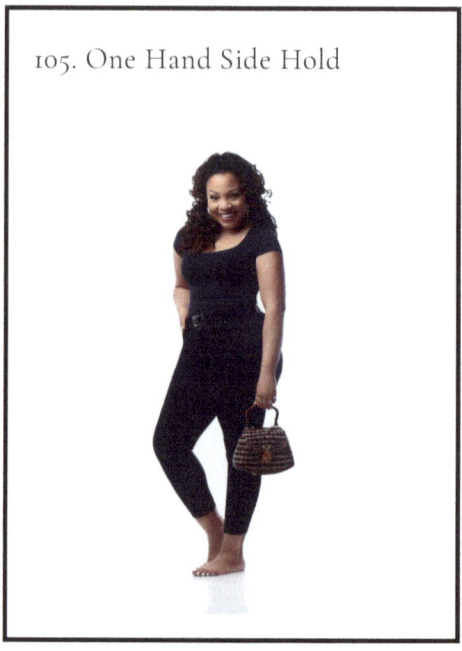

106. Wrist Loop

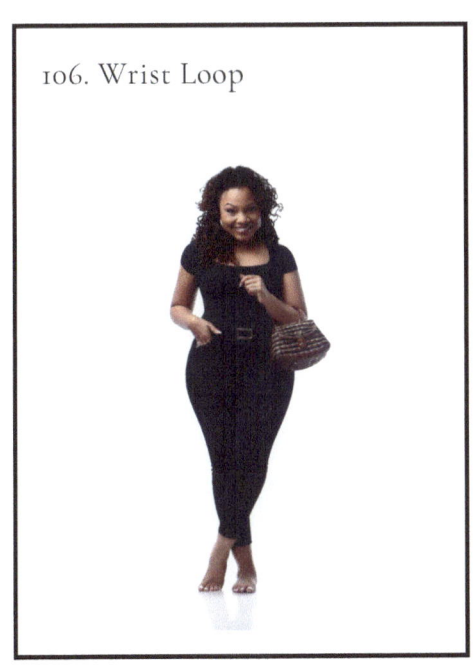

107. High-N-Mighty

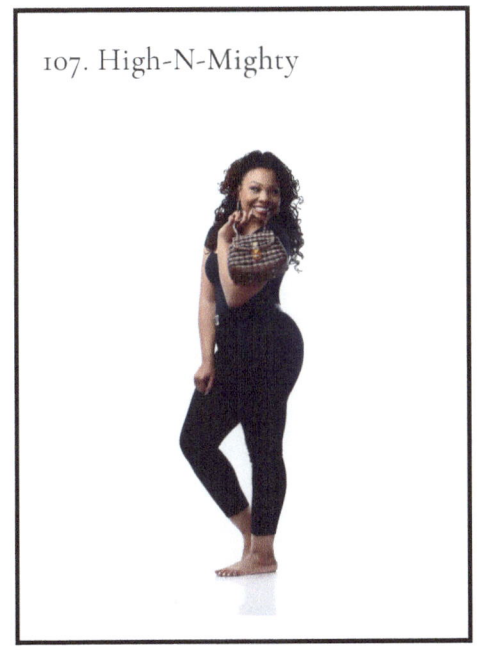

108. One Hand In Front, One Hand In Pocket/Belt Loop

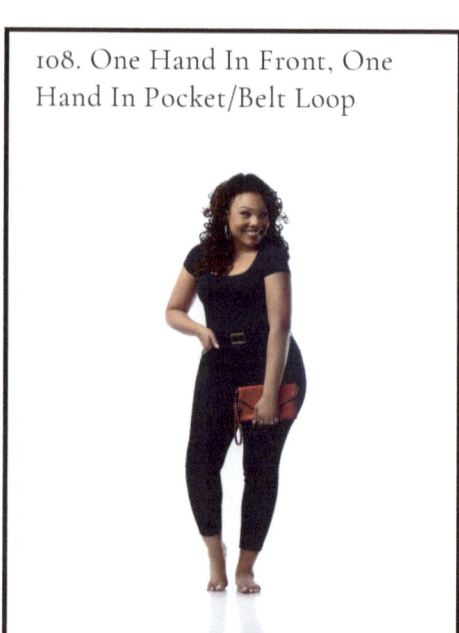

109. One Hand Side Hold, One Hand In Pocket/Belt Loop

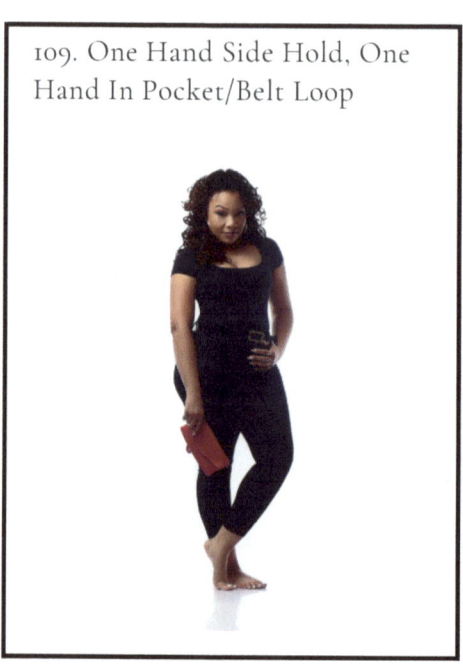

110. Front Forward Two Hands

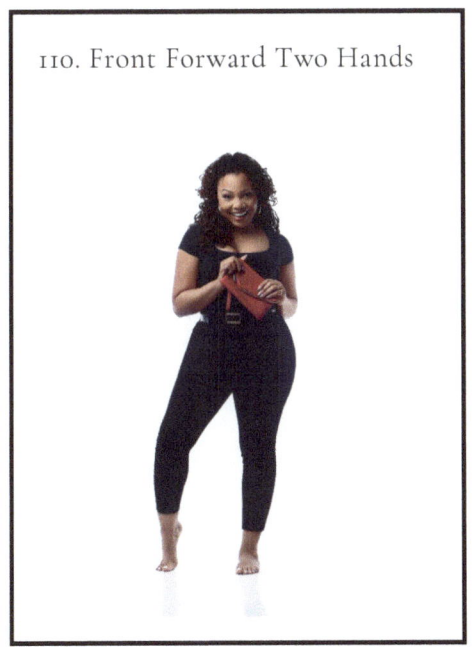

Baby Got Hacks

→**Dress for your body type:**
- Triangle (Inverted): Bring the focus up top with fun colors or statement tops and pair them with flowy skirts or pants that slim your hips.
- Rectangle (Athletic): Add some curves with ruffles, wrap dresses, or belts that cinch your waist.
- Apple (Round): Balance your shape by keeping tops simple and rocking bottoms with flare, like A-line skirts or wide-leg pants.
- Hourglass (Curvy): Show off your waist with wrap dresses, fitted tops, or high-rise jeans that hug your curves.
- Pear (Oval): Look longer and leaner with V-necklines, flowy dresses, or tops that glide over your curves.

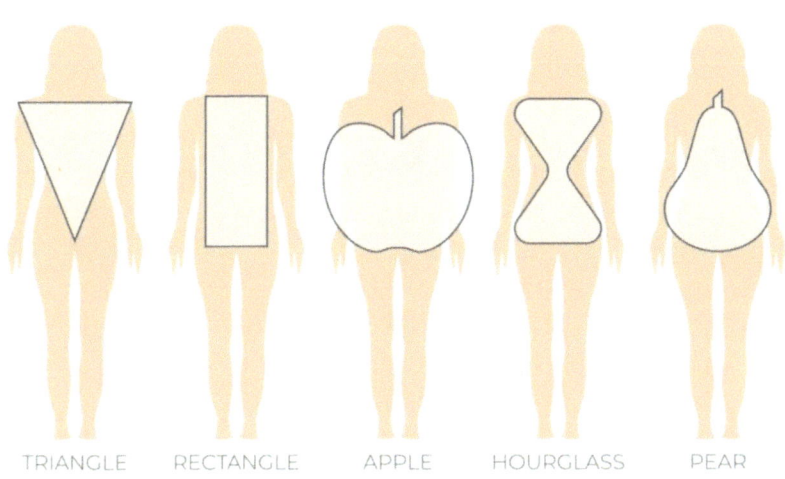

→**Create a playlist to share with the photographer that puts you in the best, confident mood**
Whether you need an additional hype man or you want to bring out that inner sexy, music is proven to put you in whatever mood you're aiming for.

→**Plan and prepare**
I've witnessed so many in their own heads before the shoot has started. By the time they stand on the backdrop, they're defeated. As experts, we understand where you need assistance (most times instantly). Allow us to guide you towards greatness during our time together. After all, you came to us for a reason! Things that may help:

- Research the type of photographer you'd like to work with.
- Create a mood board. This helps you be specific about your vision. Pinterest is my BFF!
- Set up a meeting with your photographer to ensure everyone is on the same page.
- Find out where the photoshoot will be and map out travel time and factor in weather (especially if the shoot is outside).
- Hire a stylist. Allow the experts to assist in the area you may not be the strongest in.
- Do a trial with your make-up artist.
- Drink plenty of water leading up to your photoshoot.
- Eat something light and healthy prior to your shoot. This will give you the energy you need and will prevent any unwanted digestive issues.
- Get an adequate amount of rest the night before your photoshoot.

→**Don't touch your stomach unless you're expecting**
I understand why it's done, but please try not to do this. It brings attention to the area you may be self-conscious about

and can be mistaken for a maternity shoot. Please refer to alternate options in this playbook and find somewhere else to place your hands, beautiful!

→**Pointing your toes elongates your legs**
I know, it sounds crazy and may even feel crazier while doing it, but it works. Trust me! Not only will you appear taller, but your legs will appear more toned.

→**Leg/Foot crossovers while standing accentuates your curves**
This gives you more of an hourglass appearance while cinching your waist. What's not to love about this hack, right?!

→**Degrees of separation slim you out**
Try standing in front of a full-length mirror with your arms at your sides, stand straight, and THEN place your hands on your hips, separate your legs, pop your hip, and bend the knee with less weight on it. You'll instantly notice the difference. Limbs at our sides will automatically push our flesh up against each other making us appear wider. It's legit the hack of all hacks for all body types.

→**Determine if you are a smiler or a smizer**
An expert may ask at the beginning of your photoshoot, especially if they notice it once things get started. It's more than ok to let the photographer and/or creative coach know your preference - remember, this is YOUR photoshoot! You are the #1 priority - they'll adjust to you! If you're a smiler, be prepared to show your pearly whites a lot! Your cheeks may hurt, but it will all be worth it. If you feel awkward when you smile, try laughing. It looks just like a smile in photos. If you're a smizer, stare into the soul of that camera. No really, the camera should be equivalent to your crush, LOL! Also, be sure to part your lips slightly - - degrees of separation actually do wonders in this area, too!

→**Be mindful of your natural body language**
When nervous, we may tense up causing our shoulders to shrug - now we've lost our neck. We may also stop breathing (not to the point of blacking out LOL), but to where you're not blinking and you are seemingly concentrating on not looking awkward - yet you're looking every bit of awkward! This is where observing and practicing in the mirror prior to your photoshoot helps. As service providers, we can only do so much. The more comfortable you are, the more confident you'll feel and appear!

→**When in doubt, dance it out**
In my opinion, candid shots are the absolute best! Now, you'll have to loosen up a bit, but with the right song it's more than possible. Capturing you having fun will make you more relatable to your audience. It'll show you have personality and that it doesn't have to be all business, all the time.

Conclusion

And just like that - you've got 100+ poses in your back pocket and the confidence to match! Whether you're posing for a selfie, a brand shoot, or just want to show up stronger on camera, remember; it's not about perfection, it's about presence.

You don't need to change anything about yourself - you just need to own who you already are.

Need one-on-one assistance? I got you covered! On set, I curate safe spaces that will allow your creativity and confidence to shine. I provide reassurance that will keep you lifted and I bring the FUN, fun okaaaay!

I'm excited to meet y'all! Most importantly, I'm elated to share lots more secrets and hacks that exceed far beyond this book, social media, and my in person werKshops. Now grab your mirror, set that self-timer, and start practicing! And hey - if you want even more guidance or a little extra hype, come find me. I'd love to coach you through your next photoshoot, one fierce pose at a time.

Meet Chi Anderson

She discovered her love for having her picture taken at age 5. This would eventually turn into an aspiring modeling career well into her late teens. Coming from a family of traditionalists, she obtained her B.A. in Healthcare Management, an MBA in Business, and a life coach certification in Positive Psychology. She took the safe, societal route and worked in corporate for 20 years. Never having that sense of fulfillment, Chi always knew she was destined for more than continual micromanaging and a cramped cubicle.

Eventually, her little girl dreams and grown woman prayers would be her reality...

Since returning to modeling full-time, Chi Anderson has walked for dozens of fashion designers and been photographed by some of the greats! Being well versed in her craft, she created a much-needed lane (The Creative Coach, LLC), assisting clients during photoshoots/public appearances with everything from posing to managing fine details while on set. Trust and believe...you'll need her there! She's also a runway and pageant coach for the youth, helping teen girls win numerous titles and crowns around the world.

She's also an actress, voiceover talent, and influencer. She was the first official model for Brazen Boutique and has been seen on HBO Series (Betty - Season 2). She's also a Mid America Emmy recipient for a Girl Scout commercial and has been seen on dozens of Mobile (On The Run) billboards (Missouri and Illinois) just to name a few.

She's a 2x author and also THE FIRST brown girl to place in the national

FabOver40 competition as 3rd runner-up out of over 300K contestants!

Chi Anderson is the Founder of Take Care, Sis - - a 501c3 that acts as a self care sisterhood and safe haven for women 25+ who deserve a chance to reset, recharge, and refuel. These intentional events are curated to incorporate and enhance better lifestyle choices while building an accountable community of women.

Prize & Shine Foundation (Est. 2016 - Chi's first baby) was a 501c3 that offered assistance to high school senior girls with life readiness skills while celebrating their accomplishments with laptop fundraisers, scholarships, and self-care initiatives (The Doting Diva Project) for nine years.

Chi is the recipient of the following awards - - Salute To Young Leaders (The St. Louis American Foundation), Delux Power 100, Connections To Success (Tribute To Success), Made Mogul (Community Empowerment) and the Side Hustle Honors (Wilfred J. Barry Icon). She also has been featured in articles for - St. Louis American, Riverfront Times, Danii Gold Lifestyle & Entertainment, Rare Radar, New Beauty Magazine, Canvas Rebel (ATL), St. Louis Magazine and Delux Magazine.

She is Co-Owner and Operations Manager of Church Productions (a double minority-owned production company that specializes in photography and videography for corporate clients, nonprofits, and the hospitality industry. She's also the co-host of NARP (Not A Real Podcast)- a podcast that sparks limitless conversations regarding trending topics and real life scenarios. In her spare time, Chi loves to travel, dance, hike, try new restaurants, and spend time with loved ones.

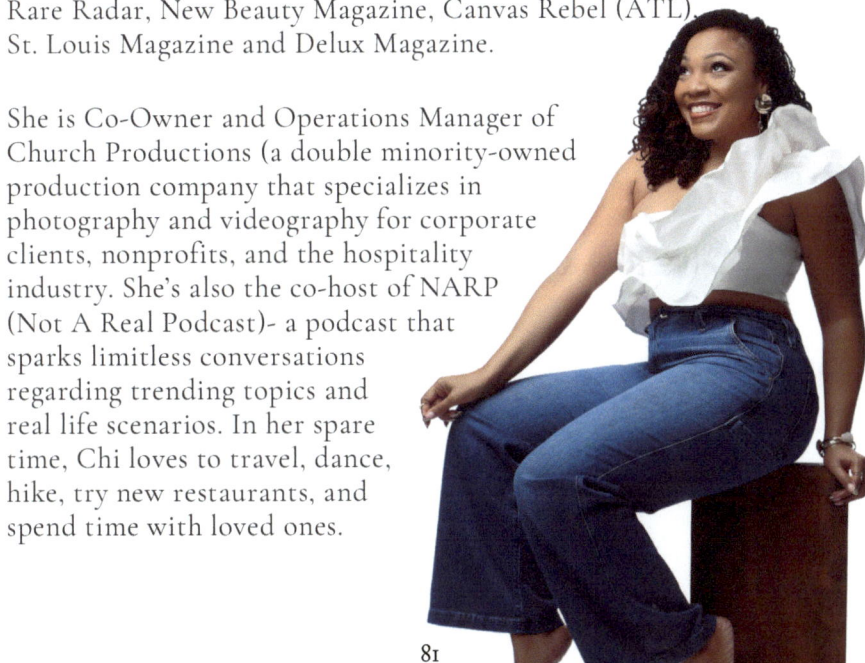

www.ingramcontent.com/pod-product-compliance
Lightning Source LLC
Chambersburg PA
CBHW040319220526
45473CB00009B/2494